I0213436

PROFESSOR DAVID HENDERSON

1927–2018

A Gedenkschrift

Copyright ©2019

All rights reserved.No part of this publication may be reproduced, stored in a retrieval system, or transmitted in any form or by any means, electronic, mechanical, photocopying, recording or otherwise, without the prior permission of the copyright holders.

ISBN 978-0-9931190-6-4

Published by The Global Warming Policy Foundation
Set in Minion.

ISBN 978-0-9931190-6-4
90000

9 780993 119064

Contents

Introduction

David Henderson is primarily, but not exclusively, known for his work on four issues:

- his pioneering analysis of the Concorde and nuclear power projects reported in his inaugural lecture as Professor of Economics at University College, London, opening the way for analysis of many ill-judged government projects;

- his 1985 Reith lectures, subsequently published as *Innocence and Design: The Influence of Economic Ideas on Policy* (Blackwell, 1986);

- the importance of economic liberalism in raising people's living standards,[*] and the *pis aller* of corporate social responsibility and what he called 'global salvationism', in incorporating ethical issues;[†]

- well argued scepticism concerning the predictions, and the consequences, of rapid global warming and the unwise and inadequate methodological approach to both When Nigel Lawson set up the Global Warming Policy Foundation, David became the first Chairman of its Academic Advisory Panel.

He was an academic of distinction at Oxford and University College, London (UCL), and, since his retirement, a visiting professor in the UK, Belgium and Australia, and a researcher and writer at the Institute of Economic Affairs. He was also an effective and well respected economic adviser in the UK Treasury, the UK Ministry of Aviation, as Director of Economics at the World Bank and the Head of the Economics and Statistics Division at the Organisation for

---

[*]See 'A New Age of Reform, Lecture given at the Annual General Meeting of the Institute of Fiscal Studies, 22 May 1989', *The Changing Fortunes of Economic Liberalism: Yesterday, Today and Tomorrow*, IEA 1998 and *Anti-Liberalism 2000: the rise of the New Millennial Collectivism*, IEA 2001.

[†]See *Misguided Virtue: False Notions of Corporate Social Responsibility* IEA 2001 and *The Role of Business in the Modern World; Progress, Pressures and Prospects for the Market Economy*, IEA 2004.

Economic Cooperation and Development (OECD). He regularly contributed, with some effect, to the correspondence columns of the *Financial Times*, especially on the appropriate use of market exchange rates and calculations of purchasing power parity in making international comparisons.

He combined rigorous analysis and deep with insight into the fruits of liberalism with an intense interest in economic policy, particularly to its intellectual foundations. Whenever I met him, he always began by asking what I was doing, continued to ask tough questions and left me with a new, or somewhat different line, of thought for the next stage. He was a brilliant teacher of economics and of the application of economic advice, an indispensible economist's economist.

He died in harness, working on the influential notion of 'market failure', an idea which he was becoming practically misleading. To our collective loss he did not have time to complete it.

Climate change, more strictly, anthropogenic global warming

This *Gedenkschrift* concentrates on David's work on climate change, reproducing two widely quoted articles in a special section of *World Economics* in 2006. David masterminded the plan for dealing with both the science and the economics and, for the latter, largely wrote a critique of the Stern Report[‡] on the economics of climate change. This was published in *World Economics* as 'The Stern Review: A Dual Critique' in two parts, both reproduced below. He had intended a final set of collective conclusions, with scientists and economists jointly signing up; unhappily, this proved impracticable.

In a subsequent edition of *World Economics*, David published an article that argued than too many economists have uncritically accepted some scientific analyses and policy prescriptions. This was a theme he used in subsequent criticisms of several international organisations including the World Bank, the International Monetary Fund(IMF) and the OECD.

[‡] *Stern Review: The Economics of Climate Change*, 2006.

Part I

Tributes

Tribute from John Henderson

Standing here today I feel a little like that character in the Marx Brothers movie, *The Cocoanuts*. This character is of course a crook and a fraudster. Naturally he is a guest of honour at a banquet, where he is invited to stand up and make a speech in front of a full gathering of assembled guests, including the Marx brothers, Margaret Dumont and the like. As he stammers away inarticulately, he admits he actually hadn't intended to make a speech at all, at which Groucho immediately interrupts 'well, you certainly succeeded'.

My sister Jane and I would like to thank you all very much for joining us this evening to celebrate the remarkable life of my father. I particularly want to thank Professor Len Shackleton from the University of Buckingham and the IEA and Dr Benny Peiser from the GWPF for co-hosting this event. We wanted it to be short, informal and definitely celebratory. From the kind and touching messages we have received from so many people, it is as clear, as it is comforting, that he seems to be as much missed by his friends as he is by his family. This is because many of you were in many ways his family also. These messages not only express regret for the loss of a remarkable man but also convey great affection. I will be reading a couple of messages from people who couldn't be here today and there are also a few people here this evening who are also kindly saying a few words.

I wanted to dwell briefly on my father's remarkable life, although some of you already know at least some of this. As a very young Oxford scholar at Corpus Christi during the war he took a first class degree in PPE and became one of Oxford's youngest dons at Lincoln. The war ended just as he was about to be asked to join Bletchley Park. As a university proctor he became heavily influential in varsity life. One of his legacies is that he persuaded doubtful Oxonians to choose the Danish architect Arne Jacobsen to design the new St Catherine's College building in the late 1950s. The distinguished architectural historian Sir Howard Colvin in his book *Unbuilt Oxford* said of my father that he was the man who did most to rescue Oxford from its architectural torpor.

He left Oxford in the early 1960s to become a Whitehall civil servant, as an economic adviser, firstly at Her Majesty's Treasury and then at the Ministry of Aviation under Roy Jenkins. He was too original a mind to want to remain either an Oxford academic or a civil servant and we subsequently travelled abroad, living in Athens, where he worked on a development project for Harvard University. Force to leave because of a military coup, we went first to Malaysia where he worked on an economic development project for the Ford Foundation and then Washington DC where he became a Director of Economics at the World Bank. Being a man of principle he disagreed so completely with the Bank's president Robert McNamara that he resigned. This was the McNamara who was Secretary of Defence under Kennedy and Johnson during Vietnam, and not someone you cross swords with lightly!

He subsequently accepted a chair in Economics at University College London in 1974. In the mid-1980s he was appointed Chief Economist at the Paris-based Organisation for Economic Cooperation and Development (OECD). In 1985 he gave the BBC Reith Lecture. For those of you who haven't had the opportunity, I would recommend his subsequent publication *Innocence and Design*, in which he beautifully describes how governments and policymakers are influenced by what he termed 'do it yourself' economic ideas. These are ideas that, while seemingly logical, are not always wise and certainly not those of economists! Margaret Thatcher became interested in his work and I remember my sister and I driving him to Chequers one Sunday in the 1980s for lunch. Although he was a great admirer of hers, he managed to successfully disagree with her also, being cross-examined by her at said lunch for over two hours!

He was still active in retirement in the early 1990s, where he had visiting chairs at Sciences Po in Paris, at the University of Melbourne, the Melbourne Business School and the Westminster Business School. Later in life, of course, he became interested in climate change and together with former Chancellor Nigel Lawson, Benny Peiser and others helped to set up the great Global Warming Policy Foundation. His disagreement with so much received wisdom about climate change and the conviction politics attached to it was characteristic of him. The fact that this flew in the face of majority popular belief did not stop him from articulately opposing broadly received opinion and doing so with meticulously researched argument and a gentleness and lack of rancour that made his case all the more powerful.

My memories (in addition to his being a marvellous father of course), is of a modest and self-effacing man. He never wanted to be called 'Professor' when he left his chair at UCL and had to be persuaded not to turn down the CMG he was awarded at his retirement. He just didn't see the point in such things. This of course belied a first class intellect and a man of true culture. He was simply interested in so many things. Not only was he a true polymath, but, luckily for all of us, one who thoroughly enjoyed sharing his wisdom. He not only loved all things cultural, in particular music, opera, jazz, architecture, literature, history, politics and different cultures, but was inevitably an expert in these fields. He was asked many years ago to give a talk on Radio 3 on jazz, as this was a particular love of his, but he characteristically refused, saying he wasn't well enough qualified. He equally loved nature and sport and enjoyed bird watching as much as a good game of rugby. He was our cultural, ethical and intellectual touchstone.

I will also remember a man who was never interested in convention or the easy path. It would surely have been easier to pursue a career as an academic at Oxford or as a rising star in the civil service. However, he left both because I think he felt there was so much more to life. He decided to travel and, in doing so, took us with him on a fantastic round-the-world adventure. We never lived as expats, always went to local schools and made many local friends. Life was never dull. In Greece we ended up being deported as a result of a military *coup d'état*, in Malaysia we found race riots between Malays and ethnic Chinese, and in the USA we found, in the late 1960s, race riots, civil rights demonstrations, anti-Vietnam war marches and political assassinations. It is hard to imagine a gentler man causing so much trouble.

I will remember a man of the highest honesty, integrity and principle. I have never known my father to lie or, the more grown up version of this, to compromise his principles regardless of consequence. We had to leave Greece after the coup, at least in part because he so strongly supported Greek politicians who opposed the military junta. He remained in contact with many of them after we left the country. He stood up to the not inconsiderable personalities of Robert McNamara and Margaret Thatcher because he believed he was right. He opposed widely accepted opinion on climate change, sometimes at some personal risk, because he believed he was right. Behind his gentleness was great courage and unbendable integrity.

I am happy to say his legacy lives on, not only in his remarkable work but also in his four wonderful grandchildren. I have a son Tom, a mechanical engineering undergraduate and talented jazz bassist, and a daughter Anna, a former British junior alpine ski race team member, going to a junior winter Olympics and more recently in the GB women's road cycling team at this summer's European championships in Glasgow and also at the World Championships in Innsbruck this September. In fact it was in Austria where I learned from my sister Jane of my father's death. Jane too has two marvellous boys, in Freddie who shows much of my father's intellect as a schoolboy at St Paul's, and in Ollie who shares so much of his originality of thinking. My father's spirit is truly well represented in them.

Tribute from Lord Lawson

David Henderson was a great man, both intellectually and morally. That is not a phrase I use lightly, let alone frequently. He combined modesty in demeanour with untrammelled intellectual integrity.

I first came across him when he gave his outstanding 1985 Reith Lectures on do-it-yourself economics, which have never been bettered and which are essential reading for any budding economist.

I next encountered him after my resignation as Chancellor in 1989. He wanted to share with me what he called his 'Appleby file', named after Humphrey Appleby of *Yes, Minister* fame. This concerned the then government's new-found obsession with the alleged threat of global warming, and its proposed solution. His file of correspondence with the senior Whitehall officials involved demonstrated a combination of ignorance and obfuscation that was indeed worthy of Sir Humphrey. David was particularly concerned that at no time was there the slightest suggestion that there should be an economic analysis of the issue.

I had by that time just been made a member of the Economic Affairs Committee of the House of Lords. David and I agreed that it might be a good thing if I could persuade my fellow members that our next enquiry should be into the economics of climate change, which I did. The ensuing unanimous all-party report was the first occasion, at least in this country, that a reasonable degree of sceptisism had been made.

I decided to follow it up by undertaking deeper research into the topic, which was published as a book, *An Appeal to Reason*, which I very properly dedicated to David.

The success of the book – which no British publisher would touch: it had to be published by an American publisher – enabled me to launch a think tank, The Global Warming Policy Foundation, which I equipped with an impressive Academic Advisory Council with, of course, David as chairman.

His contribution was immeasurable. He is greatly missed, but his legacy lives on.

Tribute from Lord Donoughue

I will talk personally about my relationship with David, as it developed through much of my long life.

I first met him in his Oxford college room in early October 1953: 65 years ago. I was to read Politics, Philosophy and Economics and he was my economics tutor at Lincoln College.

It was still post-war Britain, with ex-military men coming up as undergraduates, with food rationing, so we handed in our ration books to eat in college. I can see him now as he was then: slim, even slight, with no airs or pretensions. He felt barely older than me, and much smaller. At the beginning, I found him a little cool.

I had studied basic economics at grammar school. Although also deeply interested in poetry and the arts, I thought I might become an economics teacher. David, although always helpful, quickly and gently, and fortunately for me, put those ambitions to rest.

He was so brilliant, so clear, such a master of mathematical economics, that I realised that I could never reach those analytical, those theoretical heights. He was clearly interested in my field: what we then called 'applied economics' – such as government economic policies – but he flew so far above anywhere my modest wings might reach, that I quietly modified my ambitions to becoming just a mere don, or even just a journalist.

At first, I resented this, thinking him too dry. Completely wrong.

I soon accepted that was unfair, and that David Henderson was simply more brilliant than anyone I had until then encountered. I grew to respect, and admire, and to like him enormously, but his vast range of interests was revealed to me only slowly over the years.

I did not see much of David for some years after graduation, as our career paths parted. But in the 1970s, when I moved from teaching at LSE to advising the Prime Minister at 10 Downing Street, I often came across David at the London University and in Whitehall, where it was clear he was greatly respected as an economic adviser.

We often met and shared views. It was clear his range of interests and expertise was far broadened. Interestingly, I, a Labour peer, never knew or asked what his political party preferences were. I suspect they were never felt in party terms and were adjusted over the years as the political situation and facts changed.

He was certainly not dry. He was interested in getting government policies right, overseas as well as in Britain, while remaining committed to getting the economic facts and principles clear.

He also increasingly showed his sharp wit and humour.

Later we became much closer personally. We were both sceptics on climate change alarmism, wishing to detach the facts from the propaganda. We became involved with the GWPF, where his great role has been described by Benny Peiser. We met for lunch regularly in his favourite Indian restaurant off Piccadilly. He was intellectually sharp and witty as ever, even when losing his physical agility. He was a warm and good friend as well as a fine economist and a great national asset.

We will miss him.

Tribute from Rupert Darwall

I'd like to say a couple of words about David and his very special talent for friendship. As it happens, I first met David here at an IEA lunch. I can't remember how long ago it was or the exact occasion, but I was thrilled to meet him. And then something strange happened.

'My dear fellow, you don't believe in the triple bottom line?'

'Of course I don't.'

What was going on here? What had happened to the 1985 Reith Lecturer in the intervening years?

'But there's good money in it,' David persisted. 'You could be like John Gummer.'

In fact, this was more than a test. It was technique. David was a thoroughly accomplished wind-up artist, flinging out the latest and most outrageous examples of wrong thinking – all delivered with a straight face, but a quizzical eye to check what the reaction might be. And I have to say, in my case it worked a treat.

The result was my first book on global warming, which I started as a form of therapy from the effects of David's wind-ups. I should say it was his book as much as mine, as the terrain it traverses had been mapped out by David, informed by his extraordinary breadth of knowledge and sharp insights.

Ideas mattered to David. And I think he formed bonds with people who shared his thirst for ideas that helped one better understand the reality of the world today and, importantly to him, the past; that is to say, who shared a love of history. He had a marked distaste for bad ideas: those that confused, obscured and befuddled – and he had little time for the people who peddled them.

Age and frailty appeared to take no toll on David's appetite both for ideas and for people, always widening his circle of friends and acquaintances. In short, David was and remains, for me, an inspiration.

Tribute from Sir Ian Byatt

David Henderson was both a scholar and a practising economic adviser. He was always concerned with what was going on in policy analysis and in the technical economics, or other thinking, which lay behind economic policy. He was widely and deeply read, not only in economics: he published many books, was a prolific contributor to policy journals and gave many lectures, including the Reith lectures of 1985. He was an active networker, always reaching out to those who could help him or those he wished to influence.

I have first written about the man I knew and secondly about the contribution to policy advice contained in his writings.*

The man and his career; some recollections

I first knew David when I was an undergraduate in the 1950s, and he, a fellow of Lincoln College. I went to his lectures on control theory and the trade cycle, him teaching me about the importance of feedback and of learning from other professionals. (One test of his success was that I produced an essay for my Teddy Hall tutor, which he thought was the best, of my economics essays.) I still remember that when the lecture audience dwindled, which it always did in Oxford in those days, David invited us to informal discussions in his contemporarily furnished rooms at Lincoln.

I met him again when I joined the Economic Section of the Treasury in 1962. He had been a member of the Economic Section in the 1950s and was soon to become the Economic Adviser to Roy Jenkins at the Ministry of Aviation. He invited me to lunch at the Architectural Association.†

---

*See also David's obituaries in the *Financial Times* 9 October 2018 and the *Daily Telegraph* 25 October 2018.

†David was much interested in architecture and played a significant role in ensuring that the new St Catherine's College building was designed by a contemporary architect.

Fifteen years later, when he came back from a stint as Director of Economics at the World Bank to University College, London (UCL), and I was running the Public Sector Economic Unit in the Treasury, he asked me to give a talk on the Treasury control of nationalised industries. This was at a time when we were working on the 1978 White Paper, trying to get some financial discipline into those wayward institutions. David was, as always, sympathetic to our objectives, and judicious about our proposed techniques, involving the development of financial targets in an accounting environment.

When he was head of the Economics and Statistics Division at the Organisation for Economic Co-operation and Development (OECD) in the 1980s, when OECD was working on structural adjustment policies and we in the Treasury were working on ways to revive to the British economy through greater reliance on markets, he asked me to give a talk in Paris on economic policy. I concentrated on our supply-side work. While David valued his days at OECD, where he was mainly concerned with macro-economic policy, he also regretted the organisation's too exclusive concentration on macro-economic analysis. He wished that he had said more about this at the time.

At the turn of the century, when David had come back from Paris, and I had left Ofwat, he recruited me (his words not mine) to his campaign to preserve the liberal economy against the dangers emanating from the implementation of the environmental policies of the 1992 Rio conference. More to the point, David persuaded Nigel Lawson (now Lord Lawson of Blaby) to take the whole business seriously, first in the House of Lords, and then in founding the Global Warming Policy Foundation (GWPF). Nigel's book was appropriately dedicated to him.

David masterminded the dual (scientific and economic) critique of the Stern Report, published in *World Economics*, and widely read and quoted. He wanted to integrate the two approaches more closely; in his own words,

> I conceived the idea of twin and complementary review articles, scientific and economic; sold the idea to *World Economics* (not surprisingly, some initial persuasion was required), thus opening up the chance of prompt publication; managed all the subsequent dealings with the journal; put together an international science team which would be responsible for Part I (having already put together the economics team, as joint signatories of an earlier paper); came up with the notion of separating technical annexes from both the main texts; wrote our collective introduction to the joint critique; and combed as informal lay editor through three drafts of the science paper, in close and much-valued conjunction with Simon Scott (the opening page of Part I is my draft!). Alas, my further project for a final set of collective conclusions, with scientists and economists jointly signing up, proved impracticable.

He was the Diaghilev of the approach, choosing the actors and the theatre.

When he was at the University of Westminster he organised meetings of scientific and economic experts to discuss developments in the analysis of anthropogenic global warming, linking-up with Benny Peiser's blog. This foreshadowed the work of the GWPF, when David became the first Chairman of its Academic Advisory Panel.

David remained an active supporter of liberal political economy to the end of his life. He was no free market dogmatist; he cared about individual people and advocated the political economy framework that would both liberate and empower them. Starting on the political left, he remained a liberal[‡] to the end. He was firmly in the pragmatic tradition of Adam Smith and David Hume, and of the policy context of David Ricardo and 19th century laissez-faire, while recognising the growth in the importance of the state. In 1966,[§] David edited a book on *Economic Growth in Britain*, with contributions by other Oxford economists.[||] He wrote the chapter on 'Planning', a very cautious piece giving the arguments for and against in great detail, and concluding that economic planning has a potentially valuable role as part of a set of policies to increase the rate of growth. But it was still in the early and formative stage. What mattered was using the insights of economics to ensure efficient delivery of both individual and collective objectives.

In recent years I was lucky to have regular lunches with David; my last one, this summer, was in his donnish flat in Havanna Drive. He was always interested in what I was doing and first class at ensuring that I was on the right road, not by telling me what to do, or what to think, but in challenging my arguments by putting them in a wider context. He was extremely well read and continued to teach me about the basic elements in economics. At our last lunch, he talked illuminately about the difference between economic analysis and the analysis of changes in economic policy; one was an issue of blueprints, the other a matter of circumstances. Both were essential ingredients.

He was also a very nice and friendly man, who cared about his colleagues and his family. He was much affected by his wife's death. He managed growing physical disability with great courage and cheerfulness, never giving in. I miss him enormously, both his friendly grin and his acute brain.

[‡] I use the word liberal, as he did, in the European rather than the American sense.
[§] I am indebted to David Sawers for this.
[||] Beckerman, Foster, Opie, Scott, Streeten and Vaizey.

His writings

As an economist, David was concerned with practical results. He saw economics through the twin perspectives of freedom and prosperity. His 1985 Reith Lectures set out his vision of the role of economics in enhancing prosperity, though both macro and micro-economic policy.¶ In those lectures, which are worth reading and re-reading, he saw macro-economics as well established both in the profession and in government, while micro-economics was over-ridden both by what he called 'do-it-yourself economics' (DIYE) and by the political force of powerful pressure groups. David saw DIYE as emanating from the 'official machine of the self-contained world of Whitehall, generating its own information and ideas'. The two key economic components of DIYE were 'essentialism', the notion that some economic activities, such as manufacturing and energy sufficiency are essential to a nation's economic structure, and 'mercantilism' as the bedrock of trade negotiations. The key political concept was 'unreflecting centralism', namely that decisions, and often methods of delivery, have to be taken by government, not other economic agents.

He contrasted DIYE with conventional micro-economics, with its foundation on comparative rather than absolute costs, with adjustments at the margin, the gains from trade, on the consumer as well as the producer, working within a framework of individual decision-taking. He argued that liberalisation of the economic system within which economic agents – households, businesses and non-profitmaking organisations – operate, plus more and better use by government of these micro-economic ideas, would increase welfare through an improved allocation of resources. They would especially have the twin benefits of liberalising innovation and achieving a better allocation of investment resources.

David argued that reliance in DIYE was not only a result of concern with income distribution and economic inequality.** It rested on wider considera-

---

¶Published as *Innocence and Design: The Influence of Economic Ideas on Policy*, Basil Blackwell, Oxford 1986.

**He quoted a statement in the 1978 White Paper on Nationalised Industries (drafted by Lawrence (later Sir Lawrence Airey, the Treasury Second Permanent Secretary, Industry, at the time), that 'The government intends that the nationalised industries will not be forced into deficits by restraints on their prices. When help has to be given to poorer members of the community it will be given primarily through the social security and taxation system, and not by subsidising nationalized industry prices'. I was working on the White Paper at the time and remember that the main internal opposition to the Treasury aims to achieve a proper return to investment by nationalised industries came not from the Social Security Department but from the Departments of Energy and Prices and Consumer Protection: both of whom feared for the effects on prices of energy and consumer goods.

tions, which were as much political as economic. Political considerations were not anathema to him, just subject for analysis. He recognised that any policy analysis would involve careful consideration of the particular context of the issue. As he put it in his final Reith lecture:

> general economic reasoning is only one element in the understanding of a real-life issue or problem: and understanding, even where it can actually be achieved, is no more than a prelude to action. The action itself often has to be decided under pressure of more or less expected events.[††]

By the time that David was giving his Reith Lectures the atmosphere in Whitehall was changing. As early as the 1960s training programmes were being developed to teach administrators the elements of economics. The influx of economists during the Labour Administration of the 1960s, and the formation of a Government Economic Service (GES), responsible for professional standards, running across all Departments were beginning to bear fruit. The internal dialogue was taking place in conventional economic terms.

David was a modest man and would not have attributed much to his own influence. But he was much respected in the GES and we were much encouraged by his wisdom and his writings. He was, in the best sense of the phrase, an economist's economist.[‡‡]

Changes, of course, go in all directions, many of them unexpected. Political controversies around macro-economic issues developed in the 1970s; the clash of monetarism and Keynesianism was as much political as economic. Politics also mattered in micro-economics; the liberal stance of supply-side policies was never popular with many of those, including economists, who wanted to reform society, often by reducing the influence of money in human affairs. Nevertheless, the convention economics of resource allocation became standard analysis under New Labour.

[††] David did not believe that economists would necessarily make the right decisions. I remember talking to him about the 'Robot' proposal on the early 1950s when the government's chief economic adviser, Robert (later Lord Roberthall), defeated the proposal by 'Otto', (later Sir Richard) Clarke, a charismatic senior Treasury administrator, for the liberalisation of the exchange rate, on the grounds that it would involve higher levels of unemployment to offset inflationary pressures. Both David and I, sixty years later, believed that the jury was still out on Robot.

[‡‡] David was well known among the mandarins of Whitehall particularly for his critical analysis of big political projects, especially of the Concorde aircraft and the Second UK Nuclear Power programme. They well knew the content of his inaugural lecture at UCL. But these studies had, however little effect on the pyramid-like propensity of politicians to invent expensive successors such as the HS2 railway, a text-book example of a project looking for an objective. He and David Sawers sent written evidence to the Transport Committee of Parliament for its report on High Speed Rail. (Tenth Report – High Speed Rail. November 2011. Written evidence by David Henderson and David Sawers. HSR 200. This was duly ignored.

In his lecture to the Institute of Fiscal Studies (IFS) in 1989,* David recognised this. Since then, however, the influence of liberal economics, or more strictly the influence of liberal political economy, has waned. David saw this and tried to combat it in several books.[†]

In particular, the global warming policy since the Climate Change Act had resulted in governmental choice of investment in electricity generation followed by price controls on electricity prices. So much for privatisation! He was also a critic of Corporate Social Responsibility, regarding it as an unwelcome distraction from the role of business in a liberal economic framework and an inappropriate gift to pressure groups.[‡]

He never ceased to look around at how people were using economics. He was concerned by the development of what I call 'elective centralism'. In origin, this differs from the unreflecting centralism of the imperial bureaucrat, coming from the populist right as well as from the reforming left, arguing that government intervention was at the heart of the political contribution to economic process.

David thought that this concentration on government intervention was, in part, a result of a failure of economic analysis, resulting from a limited view of how the market economy worked, in particular though an incorrect view of competition as a state of affairs (numbers of suppliers in the market, conditions of entry, etc.), rather than a process (search for new products, market gaps, defeating rivals etc.)[§]

David viewed Keynes and Schumpeter as the two greatest economists of the 20th century.[||] He'd bought *Capitalism, Socialism and Democracy* when it was published and felt vindicated by the passage of time in his judgment of it as an important book. Although he esteemed Keynes's intellect and temperament – on more than one occasion praising how he'd deferred to a Treasury colleague who had criticised his denigration of free trade. He was dismayed at how the economics profession, thanks to its predilection for abstraction, especially into

---

*See 'A New Age of Reform? Lecture given at the Annual General Meeting of the IFS on 22nd May 1989', Fiscal Studies 1989

[†] *The Changing Fortunes of Economic Liberalism: Yesterday, Today and Tomorrow*, IEA 1998 and 'Anti-Liberalism 2000: The Rise of New Millennium Collectivism', Thirtieth Wincott Lecture 12 October 2000, The Wincott Foundation, IEA 2001.

[‡] See *Misguided Virtue: False Notions of Corporate Social Responsibility*, IEA 2001 and *The Role of Business in the Modern World: Progress, Pressures and Prospects for the Market Economy*, IEA 2004.

[§] David was immensely helpful to me when I was writing a paper, 'What of Competition and Competition Policy?', given to the Political Economy Club in May 2018.

[||] I am indebted to Rupert Darwall, author of *The Age of Global Warming; a History*, 2013 and *Green Tyranny; Exposing the Totalitarian Roots of the Climate Change Industrial Complex*, 2017.

mathematical manipulations, had lost contact with the very stuff of economic processes. In the end, this is what for him elevates Schumpeter above Keynes.

His last project, unhappily not completed before his death, was on 'market failure' where he saw many governmental policy initiatives defended on the grounds that the market was failing. If he had lived he would have pinned down the use of the idea of market failure in a thoroughly scholarly way. perhaps giving us a further chapter on DIYE, this time resulting from the electoral response of our leading politicians to events[¶] – and shown us the alternative routes of analysis that could help us to avoid this trap.

Originally published in World Economics, *19(4), October–December 2018, and reproduced with the kind permission of the editor.*

¶ Derek Scott, the economic adviser to Tony Blair told me that the biggest problem that he had was to persuade the Prime Minister that nothing needs to be done.

Tribute from Dr Benny Peiser

David was a very good friend and one of the best mentors I have had. He was also a gentle intellectual giant and a fearless fighter for truth and accuracy.

Serving as the founding chairman of our Academic Advisory Council from 2009 to 2015, David's astute mind shaped and guided the academic standards and economic rigour of the Global Warming Policy Foundation's output. He remained deeply involved in our work and activities until the last days of his active life.

In many ways, David was pivotal in the origins and founding of the GWPF. I met him for the first time about 15 years ago. At the time, I was still a university lecturer. In 1997, I had established CCNet, an international electronic network of astronomers and researchers interested in the new field of neo-catastrophism, focusing on the potential risk of near-Earth objects (asteroids and comets) of hitting our planet.

It was during the late 1990s that global warming was increasingly claimed and reported to be a global catastrophe in the making. That's when I broadened CCNet so as to encourage open and broadminded climate debates too. My old friend Julian Morris then introduced David to the network, which happily posted and distributed his articles and papers on climate economics and policy.

David had first became involved in the issue through his work with Ian Castles on the erroneous use of market exchange rates by the IPCC. That led him into a fierce battle with its then head, Rajendra Pachauri.

Around 2002/2003, David started regular meetings with fellow sceptics of climate alarmism at Westminster Business School, where he had an office. It was at these meetings that I met David.

It was David who, during those early years, convinced Nigel Lawson that an inquiry into the economic costs and benefits of global warming would be prudent, given that the Government had never looked into the economic costs of the various policies and agreements it had signed up to over the years.

In 2005, the House of Lords Economics Affairs Committee finally set up an inquiry into the economics of climate change and concluded that much of the predictions about future climate catastrophe were exaggerated and based on highly speculative models and assumptions.

Four years later, when Nigel Lawson launched the GWPF, David became the founding chairman of our Academic Advisory Council and the most active and most questioning member of our team of eminent scholars.

As chairman of the Academic Advisory Council, David assiduously scrutinised every single draft of the papers and reports we had commissioned. At the same time, he was confronted with the unrelenting harassment and attacks that were, and still are, launched at the GWPF and its principals.

When, four years ago, Sweden's eminent climatologist Professor Lennart Bengtsson resigned from our Academic Advisory Council because of unbearable pressure by some of his own climate science colleagues, David replied by highlighting that this climate of extreme intimidation was one of the main reasons for the very existence of the GWPF.

Writing to Prof Bengtsson, David said:

> Your resignation is not only a sad event for us in the Foundation: it is also a matter of profound and much wider concern. The reactions that you speak of, and which have forced you to reconsider the decision to join us, reveal a degree of intolerance, and a rejection of the principle of open scientific inquiry, which are truly shocking. They are evidence of a situation which the Global Warming Policy Foundation was created to remedy.

The GWPF would not be what is today without David's pivotal role, vital involvement and influence.

Tribute from Professor Richard Lindzen

For many years, I have been spending 4–5 months a year in Paris. It was there that a fellow climate realist, Simon Scott, introduced me to his senior colleague at the OECD, David Henderson. David seemed to me to represent an interesting combination of prudence and conviction that I came to deeply admire and value. After he returned to England, I participated in his dual critique of the Stern Report that appeared in *World Economics* where both these qualities were manifest. Subsequently, David hosted me and my wife on behalf of the Global Warming Policy Foundation a number of times. On these occasions, David displayed additional qualities. My wife, Nadine, was immensely taken by David's warmth, charm, and considerateness. Our pleasure in visiting London has been much diminished by his death. I know that we are far from alone in missing David deeply.

From David Sawers

Integrity is the word that best summarises David's character, supplemented by persistence and conviction. He could also be patient and persuasive, and had a great capacity for sheer hard work. These were the characteristics he most required in the Ministry of Aviation, which he joined as Chief Economist in 1965. He had been recruited by Roy Jenkins, who was Minister of Aviation in Harold Wilson's government of 1964, and David in turn recruited me as his deputy.

I had first met David about 1951, when I attended one or two of his lectures at Oxford. He was then 24, and already established at Lincoln College after a stellar academic career. I did not meet him again until 1963, when he had learned that I had studied the development of the aeroplane with John Jewkes. He was doing some research on the industry, and wanted to know what Jewkes and I had done. So it was not surprising that he should invite me to join him at Aviation in 1965; and, as I was finishing the book based on the earlier research, I was happy to accept.

The Ministry did not welcome David with open arms. When I told an acquaintance in the aircraft industry that I was joining the Ministry of Aviation, he said he was very glad I was going there, because he had heard that a thoroughly undesirable academic had been recruited to the Ministry. That was a time when, as John Jewkes put it, high technology was the last refuge of the enthusiastic nationalist, and opposition to high technology projects – of which Concorde was the most notorious – was widely regarded as unpatriotic. After the two advanced military projects, the TSR2 and HS1048, were cancelled to save money, the objective of the Ministry was to 'keep the design teams together' so that British military aircraft could be built in the future – if in collaboration with continental European firms.

David instead advocated collaboration with American firms and the purchase of American military aircraft, at a time when many in the Ministry of Defence building regarded the USA as the true enemy. He even arranged for an official from the Department of Defense to come to London to discuss these ideas but the visit was abortive. The visitor made the mistake of imagining that an article in the *Economist* would help, not appreciating the difference between American and British attitudes to press publicity – or that a British journalist might get his story wrong. David's proposal that the RAF should buy the American F-111 as a replacement for the TSR2 was rejected, as was collaboration between British and American firms. But the American F-4 Phantom was bought for the Navy, though refitted – at vast and unnecessary expense – with Rolls-Royce engines.

David's ideas may not have been accepted at the time, but it was little more than a decade later that the British Aircraft Corporation was discussing collaboration with Boeing – discussions which were abortive because BAC could not match Boeing's production costs. David was an accurate prophet, if he was not honoured for his views when he expounded them.

My enduring memories of working with David are the speed with which he produced well argued papers, using the old-fashioned method of writing in longhand; and the power of his arguments in discussion. He was always a highly articulate speaker. Administrators were more likely than scientists to appreciate his views. But the scientists were very influential and their attitude was well expressed by Handel Davis, then Controller of Aircraft, who once said 'I'm sure you are a very good economist, David, but...' economics does not give all the answers. His major achievement at the Ministry was to earn the respect of his colleagues, and to ensure that his opinions were heard.

David did not stay in the government service after his two year contract at Aviation finished at the end of 1966. He had been offered the new post of chief economist at the Ministry of Technology, which shows that his performance in Aviation was highly rated by the senior management. But he was unable to agree terms for the new position and moved into the international sphere and development economics.

He returned to this country in 1975, to the chair of political economy at University College. His inaugural lecture on Concorde and the Advanced Gas Cooled Reactor in 1976 brought him back to aviation and advanced technology. His name was forever linked to Concorde after this lecture, which spelt out in painstaking detail the economic costs of the Concorde and AGR programmes up to that date. His analysis was incomplete, because costs continued to mount after Concorde entered service, and the AGRs had not been completed in 1976. David did not know Concorde was dangerous as well as uneconomic, because that only became clear after it entered service. After the crash in Paris in 2000, it transpired that 57 cases of tyres bursting on take off had been recorded; though some had damaged the aeroplane, Paris was the first disaster.

The inaugural lecture did more than analyse expenditure: David gave his very perceptive views on how advanced technology should be managed. He inveighed against the disease of tidiness and urged the virtues of duplication where there is uncertainty about the what will work. His approach is widely accepted, except in the British government, where duplication still tends to be regarded as wasteful and tidiness prevails. He also suggested some ingenious methods for increasing the incentive to be right about decisions and forecasts. As he pointed out, it was unimportant to be right in the British civil service. Again, nothing seems to have changed, to judge from the disastrous decisions that the Ministry of Defence continues to make.

The breadth of David's interests sometimes produced surprises. I'd learned of his interest in, and knowledge of, architecture long ago. But it was only when he came to visit me at the seaside, and we went for a walk along the shore, that I discovered that he was a knowledgeable birdwatcher. He was able to point out and name the birds we could see on the beach, which I had often seen but could not name. One could never tell when David would display superior knowledge on obscure events; he once corrected me about the date of the battle of Tel-el-Kebir – 1883 not 1885.

His industry continued into old age. It was only two years ago that we were discussing some minor topic that might merit an article or letter, and he produced a folder with press cuttings pasted to the pages. He must have spent hours preparing such reference works.

David never gave up. His mind was always working on some current controversy, thinking whether he could get a letter into the *Financial Times* about it, or whether he should tap the knowledge of his 'mates' about it. He had an unerring eye for the absurd, such as the Government Economic Service's assumption that any divergence from perfect competition was evidence of market failure, which could justify government intervention. He always wanted to secure rational and sensible economic analysis of policy: his was the voice of reason.

Tribute from Professor Len Shackleton

David was an old-fashioned economist, and none the worse for it. He was trained in the economic classics, and was not a mathematician or econometrician; nor did he want to be. But he had a ruthlessly logical mind, a clarity of vision and a gift for written exposition, characteristics which he maintained right to the end of his life.

I first met David fifteen or sixteen years ago, when he was already in his mid-70s. He had returned from his spells in New Zealand and Australia and was without a current academic affiliation. Given his connections with the Institute of Economic Affairs, he had somehow moved in and bagged a desk, where he would regularly come in and work.

Then as now, the IEA's Lord North Street building was crowded, and Philip Booth approached me to see if I could find some alternative accommodation, with the added benefit of an academic connection. At that time I was Dean of Westminster Business School, a large school with several thousand undergraduate and postgraduate students and a growing research culture.

So David and I were introduced formally (we may have previously met at some IEA event, but my memory is hazy) in order to see if something would be possible.

This was around the time when David was working on the slippery concept of corporate social responsibility, the unintended consequences of which are still plaguing us. I had read his 2001 IEA publication *Misguided Virtue* and found myself in agreement with virtually every word. He, on the other hand, knew some of the work I had done on the remorseless spread of employment regulation and was enthusiastic about my critical take on this. So we hit it off intellectually and I arranged for him to be appointed as a visiting professor. David was living within walking distance of our Marylebone Road headquarters, so it was a convenient arrangement.

He moved into an office on the second floor, and soon became an active participant in the life of the school, regularly attending and contributing to our twice-weekly research seminars, sometimes inviting along friends such as Geoffrey Owen to talk. Although few of my Westminster colleagues, many drawn from fuzzy management disciplines rather than economics, were initially in sympathy with his views, David's intellect and friendly manner were soon accepted as a valuable contribution to the school. He was involved in other ways, attending school events, always happy to read and comment on drafts of other people's work, and even willing on occasion to turn out to invigilate undergraduate examinations.

I left Westminster at the beginning of 2008. David continued his involvement for a number of years, although his visiting professorship had elapsed, until the second or third dean following me decided that the expanding school needed his room for a full-time academic. David subsequently moved to the Global Warming Policy Foundation.

We had, however, continued to remain in close touch while I was at the University of East London. When I moved to Buckingham, I took up the editorship of *Economic Affairs,* and David became a keen contributor, referee and advisor. In particular we published a valuable correspondence, which David initiated, on comparing real GDP across countries. This attracted contributions from an ex-World Bank colleague, Jean Baneth, and Harvard's Larry Summers.

In recent years, David and I continued to correspond frequently by email and telephone, and met up for lunch. His last communication with me was to propose a new article for *Economic Affairs* on the concept of 'market failure', something which he saw as being intimately associated with the loose and sloppy thinking he had contested all his adult life. Sadly the article was never completed.

I have an inscribed copy of *Innocence and Design* in front of me. In this book, based on his Reith Lectures, David developed the idea of 'Do-it-yourself economics', his description of the flawed thinking of civil servants, politicians and other policy-makers. If I could turn that round a little, David himself was a 'do-it-yourself' economist, in a very different sense. Faced with the stultifying nonsense preached at us every day, he was prepared to take on the collectivist orthodoxies which increasingly rule our lives. While he hoped for support from the rest of us, he was prepared single-handedly, from mid-career to an advanced age, to assert the continued relevance of classical liberalism. He really did it himself, and for that we should be very thankful.

Part II

David's lasting contribution to the climate debate

The Stern Review: A Dual Critique

Originally published in *World Economics*, October–December 2006.

Authors' introduction

The twin papers that follow present a critique in two parts of the Stern Review on *The Economics of Climate Change*. Part I focuses on scientific issues and their treatment in the Review. It forms the point of departure for Part II which deals with economic aspects.

The Stern Review was commissioned in July 2005 by the UK's Chancellor of the Exchequer, Gordon Brown. It was conducted under the joint auspices of the Cabinet Office and the Treasury, and the final text was delivered to the Chancellor and the Prime Minister who both spoke at its launching at the end of October 2006. Sir Nicholas Stern is Head of the Government Economic Service in the UK and Adviser to the British government on the economics of climate change. Although the Review was commissioned and financed by Her Majesty's Government, and largely drafted by British officials, it is described as 'independent'.

The Review is a formidable document. Its main text comprises over 550 pages, and covers or refers to a vast range of issues. It reflects the work of a team of over 20 officials under the direction of Sir Nicholas, backed by a substantial number of consultants. It draws on an array of already published studies and papers, as well on a substantial number of specially commissioned outside contributions. In dealing with the economic aspects which form its main concern, it develops a closely constructed argument of is own. On the basis of what it takes to be established science, together with its own distinctive analysis of the economic issues, it draws strong and confident conclusions for policy.

The Review has been widely hailed as an authoritative guide to thinking and policy. It is seen as providing an accurate account of generally agreed and increasingly disturbing scientific conclusions, and as building on these, through solid economic reasoning, an unassailable case for far-reaching and immediate collective action to limit and reduce emissions of 'greenhouse gases' in general and CO_2 in particular. To quote the British Prime Minister, at the launch of the Review,

> ...what is not in doubt is that the scientific evidence of global warming caused by greenhouse gas emissions is now overwhelming...[and]...that if the science is right, the consequences for our planet are literally disastrous...what the Stern Review shows is how the economic benefits of strong early action easily outweigh any costs.

In what follows, we take issue with such assured and unqualified verdicts. In relation to both scientific and economic issues, we question the accuracy and completeness of the Review's analysis and the objectivity of its treatment. We thus present a critique of the Review, rather than a full assessment of the argument as a whole.

The subject of the Review is the economics of climate change, and its terms of reference did not require it to cover scientific aspects. However, the text carries substantial sections on these; and it is on the basis of what scientific inquiry is taken to have established that the Review adopts as its starting point for the economic analysis that 'climate change...is the greatest and widest-ranging market failure ever seen'. The credibility of the Review as a whole thus depends in large part on what it says or presumes about 'the science'. Hence this critique, though it appears in an economic journal, has a scientific as well as an economic dimension.

The analysis that we present below, and the views that we express, are ours alone: they should not be attributed to any of the various institutions that we are affiliated with. We represent no interests, and we have neither sought nor received any financial or institutional support for our work. We write as independent commentators.*

---

* Details of the authors are to be found at the end of the article. The idea of a dual critique, with twin papers authored respectively by scientists and economists, originated with David Henderson, who has played the leading part in bringing it to fruition.

Part I: The science

Robert M. Carter, C. R. de Freitas, Indur M. Goklany, David Holland & Richard S. Lindzen

Introduction

The Stern Review includes an introductory chapter that summarises the present state of climate science and, in Part II, an analysis of the physical and environmental impacts of prospective future paths of climate change. The credibility of the document as a whole thus rests in large part on how far the material presented under these two science headings is accurate and balanced.

Two distinct aspects are relevant here. First, there is the question of whether it can indeed be said, as the Review asserts in its opening sentence, that

> The scientific evidence is now overwhelming: climate change presents very serious global risks, and it demands an urgent global response.

Second, there is the related issue of how far the Stern Review, in the sections that it devotes to them, gives an accurate account of the scientific issues.

We consider that the Review is doubly deficient. The scientific evidence for dangerous change is, in fact, far from overwhelming, and the Review presents a picture of the scientific debate that is neither accurate nor objective.

We present our argument under three main headings. In Section 1 we consider the Review's treatment of basic issues of climate science, and its overconfident conclusions about the prospective course of 'greenhouse gas' concentrations and global warming. In Section 2 we turn to what the Review says about the prospective impacts of the climate changes that it envisages as possible or likely. Under both headings, we note two interrelated features of the Review: First, that it greatly understates the extent of uncertainty, for there are strict limits to what can be said with assurance about the evolution of complex systems that are not well understood. Second, that its treatment of sources and evidence is selective and biased. These twin features combine to make the Stern Review a vehicle for alarmism.

Section 3 is concerned with fundamental issues of scientific conduct and procedure that the Review fails to consider. Professional contributions to the climate change debate very largely take the form of published peer-reviewed articles and studies. It is widely assumed, in particular by governments and the Intergovernmental Panel on Climate Change (IPCC), that the peer review process provides a guarantee of quality and objectivity. This is not so. We note that the process as applied to climate science has tolerated gross failures in due disclosure and archiving, and that peer review is both too inbred and insufficiently thorough to serve any audit purpose, which we believe is now essential for science studies that are to be used to drive trillion-dollar policies.

Besides these three main sections and our summary conclusions in Part 4, we comment in an annex on some aspects of the mishandling of data in the Stern Review. Overall, our conclusion is that the Review is flawed to a degree that makes it unsuitable, if not unwise, for use in setting policy.

1. Flaws in the alarmist paradigm

The alarmist view of climate science

Sir Nicholas Stern made a revealing comment in his OXONIA lecture of January 2006: 'in August or July of last year, [he] had an idea what the greenhouse effect was but wasn't really sure'.[1] It seems that, starting from a position of little knowledge of the issues, he has swiftly espoused the official view of the Hadley Centre for Climate Prediction and Research, on whose advice the Review relies heavily. But this Hadley Centre picture of reality, though broadly in line with that of the IPCC, is by no means universally held. Many of the specific claims that are endorsed in the Review have been seriously challenged in the scientific literature, while the text plays down the great uncertainties that remain.

The Hadley message, as reflected in the Review, is an alarmist one. It presumes without question that moderate further increases in atmospheric CO_2 levels will give rise to major climatic changes and that these are likely to be seriously damaging; that the climatic changes observed over recent decades can be reliably blamed on emissions of 'greenhouse gases' in general, and CO_2 in particular; and that climate model projections and forecasts present a sufficiently accurate view of the future at relevant geographic and temporal scales to form a basis for major policy decisions.

The Stern Review itself fails to take proper account of the profound uncertainties and major gaps in knowledge of climate science, and neither does it address the many continuing debates regarding climate change mechanisms and impact assessments. Like its sources, the Review gives unwarranted credence to model projections over firmly established data and findings. By exaggerating climate alarm it focuses on implausible rather than likely outcomes, and thereby fails to provide a sound basis for policy.

Mishandling of uncertainty

The Review states on page 10 that: 'The analysis of climate change requires, by its nature, that we look out over 50, 100, 200 years and more. Any such modelling requires caution and humility, and the results are specific to the model and its assumptions. They should not be endowed with a precision and certainty that is simply impossible to achieve.'

Yet in this respect the Review repeatedly fails to heed its own warning. The tone is set by the Executive Summary which announces without qualification that 'These concentrations [of greenhouse gases] have already caused the world to warm by more than half a degree Celsius and will lead to at least a further half degree warming over the next few decades, because of the inertia in the climate system.' This is only the first of dozens of unqualified Review statements that attribute causality or state what 'will' happen to climate or the biosphere.

A prime element of this unwarranted certainty is the Review's confidence in computer model outputs. Indeed, the Review gives these outputs even more credence than the IPCC, which warned in its Third Assessment Report (TAR) of 2001 that:

> In climate research and modeling, we should recognize that we are dealing with a coupled non-linear chaotic system, and therefore that *the long-term prediction of future climate states is not possible*. The most we can expect to achieve is the prediction of the probability distribution of the system's future possible states by the generation of ensembles of model solutions.[2]

The IPCC has highlighted the process whereby uncertainty accumulates throughout the process of climate change prediction and impact assessment [which] has been variously described as a '*cascade of uncertainty*' (Schneider, 1983) or the '*uncertainty explosion*' (Henderson-Sellers, 1993)'.[3] There are many levels of cascaded uncertainty, each one contributing to the overall uncertainty. These cascades of uncertainty extend from estimates of relevant location-specific climatic changes to their biophysical and socioeconomic impacts.

The Review attempts to deal with these uncertainties by comparing thousands of model runs under varying assumptions. The model parameterisation chosen takes no account of the possibility that carbon dioxide emissions may have minor or benign effects, and is slanted towards emphasis on larger impacts, feedbacks and damages than even the IPCC has implied to date.

In arguing that the Review has misread the state of the science, we shall challenge some of its specific assertions on climatic mechanisms. In doing so, we do not deny the possibility of future climate risks, especially from natural climate change; nor do we argue that models should only be used if they are able to meet an unrealistic standard of perfection, for their main value is heuristic, not predictive. But we do assert that it is misleading of the Review to draw so predominantly from the upper end of risk distributions and then present these as representative of the range of credible outcomes.

Climate prediction: is it a mature or a new science?

Some of the unjustified confidence in the Review appears to derive from a perception that climate prediction is a mature branch of science with a pedigree of unchallenged research dating back to work by Fourier in 1827.[4] The reality is that climate prediction, far from being a mature science, is a new area that has emerged from the science of weather forecasting, aided by the dramatic increase in power and availability of computers in the last three decades. In its last Assessment Report, the IPCC still rated the 'level of scientific understanding' of nine out of twelve identified climate forcings as 'low' or 'very low',[5] highlighted the limitations and short history of climate models,[6] and recognised large uncertainties about how clouds react to climate forcing.[7] Since then, major scientific papers have claimed, among other things, that the forcing of methane has been underestimated by almost half,[8] that half the warming over the twentieth century might be explained by solar changes,[9] that cosmic rays could have a large effect on climate,[10] and that the role of aerosols is more important than that of greenhouse gases.[11] Generally speaking, none of these suggestions is included in current climate models though, as mentioned later, aerosols are used, without any proper or rigorous basis, to cancel greenhouse warming which would otherwise be far in excess of what we have experienced. Moreover, given the estimated temperature change over the late twentieth century amounted to only a few tenths of a degree, there must be significant doubt as to whether model simulations of external forcings are even required as an explanation. Such minor fluctuations may rather be due to natural, internal, unforced variability. The primary sources of this natural variability are oceans that are never in equilibrium with the surface (because of irregular and poorly understood exchanges between the huge abyssal heat reservoir and the thermocline), together with a turbulent and heterogeneous atmosphere where changing circulation deposits heat in regions with differing infrared opacity. It may be many decades before models can account for this level of complexity, if it ever proves possible.

Exaggerating warming trends

Early in the OXONIA Technical Annex, it was said with unjustified certainty that 'The rate and scale of 20th century warming has been unprecedented for at least the past 1,000 years.' While the Review backtracks somewhat,[12] the claim raises the issue of context. We have at most a 50-year span of accurate global measurements of temperature and greenhouse gases. Meaningful judgements about climate change and, in particular, natural variations, cannot be made based on such a trivially short time span; even 1000 years is short on the climatic time scale.

The only genuinely global records of measured temperature come from weather balloon radiosonde measurements (since 1958) and satellite microwave sounding units (since 1978). These data, for what they are worth over such short time periods, indicate a gentle warming trend of about 0.1–0.2 degrees C/decade.[13] On a century scale this is at the low end of the trends the Review considers. Moreover, much of the increase in the balloon data is associated with a single step-like event in 1976–77. In the post-1979 interval, the most recently revised satellite data show little change, especially in the tropics and Southern Hemisphere.[14] The trend, such as it is, is at least in part an artifact caused by irregularities such as volcanic eruptions and El Nino events,[15] and anyway – prima facie – it is unalarming in both rate and magnitude. Nor is there any sign of acceleration either in surface or tropospheric data, calling into question the Review's emphasis on outcomes involving decadal trends of 0.3–0.6 degrees C. Despite the accumulation of CO_2 in the Earth's atmosphere since 1900, and especially since 1950, no global temperature databases exhibit temperature trends of such magnitude. The rates of modern temperature change observed fall well within the rates of minor warmings and coolings inferred for the Holocene in, e.g., the GRIP ice core.[16]

If comparison is made with the 'global average temperature' statistic since 1860 that is computed from near-surface thermometer measurements,[17] then the *late twentieth-century warming is similar in both amount and rate to an earlier (natural) warming between 1905 and 1940.* Comparisons over longer and more climatically relevant time spans have to be made using local proxy datasets. The best such datasets come from ocean seabed and polar ice cap drill cores. For example, the oxygen isotope (proxy air temperature) record from the Greenland GRIP drilling project shows that the late twentieth-century warming represents an intermittent high on a sinusoidal, millennial temperature pattern[18] of possible solar origin.[19] *This record shows that recent warming occurred at a similar rate, but was of lesser magnitude than the earlier, millennial warmings associated with the Mediaeval, Roman and Minoan warm periods.*

Thus the Review's apodictic claim that 'An overwhelming body of scientific evidence indicates that the Earth's climate is rapidly changing, predominantly as a result of increases in greenhouse gases caused by human activities'[20] is without foundation.

Reinventing climate history

Public and governmental concerns over anthropogenic global warming (AGW) soared with the intense and, until recently, continuous media use of a single graph from the IPCC's Third Assessment Report of 2001. This diagram, originally taken from papers in 1998 and 1999 by Mann *et al.*,[21] showed nine centuries of near constant global temperatures followed by a dramatic rise in the twentieth century correlating with the rise in CO_2 concentrations. The Mediaeval Warm Period (MWP), previously believed significantly warmer than now, and the much colder Little Ice Age (LIA) did not appear on this graph, which was dubbed the 'hockey stick' (owing to the shape of its curve) soon after its publication and became the basis of claims that natural climatic variation had been very small for a thousand years.

Other scientists have undertaken temperature reconstructions that are said in the Review to corroborate the 'hockey stick', but overlap in the proxies and methods used in these reconstructions casts doubt on their independence. For many, from various disciplines, from the outset the implications of the 'hockey stick' appeared unlikely. Historians and other scientists had documented the LIA, with its frozen Thames, and the flowering of civilizations in the MWP. Taken at face value, these lines of evidence[22] suggest that natural factors played a far more significant role in climate changes than the 'hockey stick' reconstruction suggested. They put in question claims that recent warmth can only be explained by human-induced increases in greenhouse gases.

Despite implying that the debate on the science of climate change is now settled, the Review had no choice but to admit that major doubts exist over the 'hockey stick'. Two recent US reports, one by the National Research Council (NRC) and one by Edward Wegman, Chair of the National Academy of Sciences Committee on Applied and Theoretical Statistics, have invalidated the 'hockey stick' conclusion.[23] These reports have confirmed earlier findings that the hockey-stick shape is an artifact resulting from a combination of defective statistical methods and inclusion of data on bristlecone pine tree-rings, which have been demonstrated to be unreliable as temperature proxies.[24]

While previously the 'hockey stick' study was presented as proof of human-induced climate change, the Review now says in Box 1.1 (our emphasis) 'Climate change arguments do not rest on 'proving' that the warming trend is unprecedented over the past Millennium. *Whether or not this debate is now settled,* this is only one in a number of lines of evidence for human induced climate change.' However, page 6 then adds that (our emphasis) 'Much of the debate over the attribution of climate change *has now been settled* as new evidence has emerged to reconcile outstanding issues.' The Review fails to specify this 'new evidence' but in any case, attribution studies can never be 'evidence': they are heuristic thought experiments designed to explore possibilities, not provide definitive explanations. Some further problems with such studies are discussed below.

While earlier Stern Review documents cited the 'hockey stick' as valid evidence[25] – which it is not – the Review now treats it as irrelevant. But this also is not a tenable position. Climate models are tuned to the low estimate of natural climate variability put forward by the IPCC in 2001. Were it proved that the world was much warmer in mediaeval times, the models could not replicate this without giving more weight to natural variability and, perforce, their ability to identify anthropogenic forcing would be decreased.

Attribution studies: circular reasoning

The Review's confidence that greenhouse gases are likely to give rise to major, deleterious climate change appears to be based in large measure on the results of a single Hadley Centre paper prominently used in the IPCC WG1 Third Assessment Report.[26] However, as can be seen from the Assessment Report, in order to simulate observed trends in global mean surface temperature, the Hadley Centre had to eliminate about two-thirds of the anthropogenic greenhouse forcing with countervailing aerosols (the net result being referred to as anthropogenic forcing). That is to say, the model – like others of its kind – exaggerates the actual warming which was only a few tenths of a degree. Further, as leading researchers in aerosol science reported in *Science*,[27] the aerosol forcing is so poorly known that they felt that calculating how much aerosol forcing is needed to cancel greenhouse forcing is as good a way of estimating the aerosol forcing as any. At the same time, the IPCC's use of this level of uncertainty to claim that the model had simulated observations is self-evidently circular. In actuality, even the sign of aerosol forcing is unknown. In a more rational and less politicized environment, one would at least entertain the simplest resolution of the problem: namely, that the models are exaggerating the response to anthropogenic greenhouse forcing.

The circular reasoning that characterizes attribution studies based on deterministic modeling of presumed forcings undermines claims that they prove warming could only be caused by those forcings. Former Director of Research at the Royal Netherlands Meteorological Institute, Dr Hendrik Tennekes[28] recently pointed out that:

> [T]hose that advocate the idea that the response of the real climate to radiative forcing is adequately represented in climate models *have an obligation to prove that they have not overlooked a single nonlinear, possibly chaotic feedback mechanism that Nature itself employs* ....[T]he task of finding all nonlinear feedback mechanisms in the microstructure of the radiation balance probably is at least as daunting as the task of finding the proverbial needle in the haystack.

Even the IPCC cautioned in relation to the Hadley attribution study that 'These results show that the forcings included are sufficient to explain the observed changes, *but do not exclude the possibility that other forcings may also have contributed.*[29] The Review, however, disregards these warnings and flatly asserts that 'more than a decade of research and discussion…has reached the conclusion there is *no other plausible* explanation for the observed warming for at least the past 50 years'.[30]

Although the Review neither mentions nor discusses them, several other plausible explanations of recent warming have been advanced in the professional literature. One line of research has correlated recent temperature trends with local heating caused by urbanization and industrialization.[31] Other studies using longer-term geological evidence also suggest minimal impacts from greenhouse gas forcing. One of these concludes that:

> …the global warming observed during the latest 150 years is just a short episode in the geologic history. The current global warming is most likely a combined effect of increased solar and tectonic activities and *cannot be attributed to the increased anthropogenic impact on the atmosphere.* Humans may be responsible for less than 0.01°C (of approximately 0.56°C total average atmospheric heating during the last century).[32]

The Review fails to refer to any of this research, the very existence of which contradicts claims that the science is settled or that GHG forcing is needed to explain current warming. It also fails to notice that models trained to emulate climate using both the instrumental record and longterm geological evidence – e.g. the last 140 years of surface temperature measurements,[33] the last 5,000 years of proxy climate data from a Caribbean marine core and a South African speleothem,[34] or the 100,000 year-long GRIP ice core[35] – are not only successful in 'predicting' the current warming phase, but also suggest cooling over the next few decades. This conclusion has also recently been strengthened on a more analytical basis by NASA and the Russian Academy of Sciences, both of which have issued predictions that cooling will occur early in the twenty-first century as solar activity decreases.

Carbon dioxide in perspective

It is important to distinguish CO_2 emission levels, CO_2 concentrations in the atmosphere, and climate forcing. It is the last that is directly relevant to the purported problem of warming. Emission reductions proposed by the Kyoto Protocol would have only a minuscule effect on atmospheric concentrations, while increments in these concentrations would anyway have a diminishing impact on climate forcing. A doubling of CO_2 is used as a benchmark for climate sensitivity and represents a forcing of about 3.7 Watts per square meter. Since anthropogenic greenhouse forcing is already estimated at about 2.7 Watts per square meter – a little over half due to CO_2, with about half of the rest to methane – then in terms of climate forcing, we are already about three quarters of the way to an effective doubling of CO_2, yet we have experienced much less warming than such forcing would suggest. *The Review assumes, against all empirical evidence and physical reasoning, that future increments of CO_2 will have substantially greater effects than those in the past.*

Changes in the CO_2 concentration are not well correlated with the 0.6 degree C increase exhibited by the surface thermometer 'global average temperature' estimates during the twentieth century. First, the phase of temperature increase between 1905 and 1940 occurred before any greatly increased industrial emissions of CO_2. Second, the rapid post-1940 increase in CO_2 emissions was accompanied by a falling temperature between 1945 and 1965. The hockeystick curve had the striking property that its heavy smoothing and axis-scaling visually diminished these matching problems, and led to a much more plausible-looking match between the alleged temperature changes and actual CO_2 curves. Even the direction of causality is open to question. Data from ice cores indicate that, during ancient climate changes, increases in temperature preceded parallel increases in CO_2 by at least hundreds of years.[36]

This brings us to the matter of feedbacks. It is generally calculated that a doubling of CO_2 would, other factors kept constant, result in a global mean warming of about 1 degree C. Alarming predictions all require that water vapour and clouds act so as to greatly amplify the impact of CO_2. But it is freely acknowledged, including by the IPCC, that water vapour and especially clouds are poorly modelled, while the underlying physics for determining their behaviour is missing or even unknown. The governing equations of fluid dynamics (Navier-Stokes) have resisted solution for over 100 years; indeed the Clay Institute is offering a $1 million prize to anyone who can merely prove a solution exists. The Review's glib treatment of this fundamental issue again spotlights its failure to grasp the uncertainty of climate research.

The Review's only substantive remarks on water vapour feedback[37] turn out to be irrelevant. These relate to Lindzen's 1990 suggestion for a mechanism whereby a warmer surface might lead to a drier tropopause region, even though it has long been shown that changes in water vapour at these levels would have marginal impact on climate.[38] To be sure, water vapour near the surface (where the bulk of the atmosphere's water vapour is found) is also relatively unimportant. Rather, it turns out that water vapour near the middle of the troposphere dominates this feedback. Thus, the 2005 Soden reanalysis of trends in upper atmosphere water vapour,[39] which the Review advances as a definitive refutation of Lindzen's 1990 suggestion, does not relate to any important feed-

43

back. More important, it has long been noted that the water vapour and the related cirrus cloud distribution are extremely spatially heterogeneous with distinct moist/cloudy and dry/clear regions. The restriction to clear regions (as is, in fact, done in Soden's study) is unlikely to be meaningful on this count either. For some time now it has been recognized that the real feedback in the atmosphere likely consists in simply changing the relative areas of moist/cloudy and dry/clear regions.[40] Much recent work supports the existence of such a mechanism, the strength of such a mechanism, and the failure of current models to replicate the data from which such conclusions emerge.[41] Much new research is currently in progress. The process (sometimes referred to as the Iris Effect), it should be noted, would reduce sensitivity to a doubling of CO_2 to less than 0.5 degrees C – rather more consistent with observations.

The Review is too confident and unqualified in assigning an overriding role to greenhouse gases in determining climate. Its approach ignores observational facts and cherry-picks among papers that promote alarm.

2. Overstating climate impacts

The same pattern of alarmism is apparent in the Review's treatment of climate impacts, for these impacts are made to appear dire by the introduction of two systematic biases. The first is the choice of scenarios. The studies of impacts used in the Review are based largely on four of the 40 scenarios developed by the IPCC.[42] They thus omit two of the six 'illustrative' scenarios chosen by the IPCC as 'equally sound'.[43] The missing scenarios are both from the A1 'very high growth' family: A1B (Balanced) and A1T (predominantly non-fossil fuels). The only A1 scenario used by the Review is the extreme A1FI (fossil fuel intensive) scenario,[44] which yields a central estimate of warming in the twenty-first century of 4.33°C, compared to 2.79°C for scenario A1B and 2.38°C for A1T.[45]

In addition to focusing on the highest of three emissions scenarios that assume rapid global economic growth and ignoring the other 'very high' economic growth scenarios that yield much lower warming projections, the Review selects IPCC scenario A2 as its base case.[46] This scenario projects global population in 2100 at 15 billion.[47] But according to the International Institute for Applied Systems Analysis, there is only a 2.5% probability that world population will exceed 14.4 billion in 2100.[48] Thus, the A2 population projection is considered highly unlikely by the research institute that prepared it. This is not surprising, since the A2 estimate for 2100 is more than 50% above the UN's latest medium population scenario and 7% above its high scenario.[49] This inflated population estimate inflates emissions and, more important, the numbers at risk for each of the climate-sensitive hazards examined in the Review, and hence the consequences and costs of dealing with them.

A second systematic bias in the Review's consideration of climate impacts is its reliance on papers that assume either that human beings will take no countermeasures to combat adverse impacts of climate change, or that any measures they do take will utilize existing technologies. In fact, we can confidently expect improved technologies in the wealthier and more technologically advanced worlds that will eventuate, and are indeed depicted by IPCC's scenarios.

In these and other ways, the Review's consideration of various climate impacts is biased towards damaging or disastrous outcomes. Some specific examples follow.

Hunger and agricultural productivity

The studies cited by the Review under this heading can be traced mainly to a paper by Parry *et al.*[50] This study allows for some adaptations and increased use of existing technology that would improve productivity. But it explicitly excludes any technologies that may be developed specifically to cope with negative impacts of climate change.[51] This is not a sound procedure. The potential for future technologies, including biotechnology, to cope with climate change is large even in developing countries, especially given the prospective continuing increases in their per capita income. Thus, the abrupt declines in yields predicted by the Review once certain temperature thresholds are reached are unlikely given appropriate breeding, crop switching and other adaptations in the decades during which temperature might be rising towards these thresholds.[52] Most other threats to agriculture and food supply, e.g., waterlogging, drought, and salinity, have also to be weighed in the light of the obvious possibilities for adaptation.

The approach used in Parry *et al.* to estimate the impacts of climate change decades from now is – in essence – tantamount to estimating today's level of hunger (and agricultural production) based on the technology of fifty years ago. Past prognostications made along these lines have proven to be spectacularly wrong precisely because they omitted from consideration developments in agricultural technology that occurred in subsequent decades.[53]

Another source of the Review's overestimates of future levels of hunger is its treatment of the prospective fertilisation of crops by additional carbon dioxide. The Review says that, following Parry, it assumes that carbon fertilisation is 'weak' and 'smaller than previously thought'.[54] Close scrutiny of the Review's footnotes is required to descry the fact that the actual assumption is not weak fertilisation but *'no fertilisation effect'*.[55] The basis for this assumption, which flies in the face of numerous papers on the reality of carbon fertilisation, is a recent paper (Long et al., 2006), which suggests only that under field conditions, carbon fertilisation may be a third to less than half of what is suggested by experiments using growth chambers.[56] The Review's effective assumption of no carbon fertilisation, which is wholly unrealistic, allows it to make a headline projection that '250–550 million additional people may be at risk'[57] of hunger, whereas, on its own figures, an assumption of strong fertilisation would have suggested declining numbers of hungry people, even for a temperature increase of up to 3.5 degrees C.[58]

Ecosystems and extinction risks

The Review acknowledges that much of the 'information' furnished with regard to impacts on ecosystems and extinction risks that it quotes originates with Thomas et al. (2004) and concedes that there is a 'great deal of uncertainty inherent in such estimates'.[59] This acknowledgement, however, is offered only several pages after the results of the Thomas et al. study have been highlighted in the Executive Summary, and in Key Messages for Part II and Chapter 3. Moreover, the Review uses these estimates repeatedly and often without any qualification. For example, Figure 2 of the Executive Summary notes 'Many species face risk (20–50% in one study),' but it fails to note the uncertainties associated with that 'one study'. Similarly, the Executive Summary states that 'Ecosystems will be particularly vulnerable to climate change, with around 15–40% of species potentially facing extinction after only 2 °C of warming.'[60] Here, as elsewhere, the reader is not warned that this statement is based on a single study, which, moreover, is fraught with uncertainties.[61]

After finally acknowledging the substantial uncertainty associated with the Thomas et al. (2004) study, the Review attempts to justify its use by saying that 'other studies looking at climate suitability also predict high levels of extinction'.[62] But many of the problems inherent in the Thomas et al. study are also endemic to these other studies. A basic issue is whether such climate suitability studies are even able to predict extinction risks under different climatic regimes. For each such regime, atmospheric concentrations of CO_2, rates of plant growth, water use efficiency, the energy requirements of species and their predator–prey relationships would all be different from what they are today.[63] As noted by Schwartz et al. (2006), 'the efficacy of using bioclimatic models to assess the possible extinction potential of climate change, particularly among species with small distributions, requires empirical assessment', while claiming that climate change puts a particular endemic species at risk of extinction 're-quires a detailed understanding of the responsiveness to climate of the target species, as well as that of species with which it is likely to interact'.[64]

The Review also ignores what has been written about the likelihood that carbon fertilisation, and other factors likely to extend secular increases in agricultural productivity, will reduce habitat loss and increase water use efficiency of plants, thereby reducing pressures on ecosystems and biodiversity.[65] Lower habitat loss would also conserve migration corridors, something that has been advanced as a mechanism to aid species adapt to changed circumstances. Moreover, changes in forest productivity (because of higher CO_2 concentrations, for instance) would similarly promote biodiversity. Thus it is conceivable, indeed probable, that at low to moderate levels of climate change, the overall pressure on biodiversity, ecosystems and species would on balance be lower.[66] In sum, the Review's assessment of ecosystem and extinction risks are a worse-than-worst-case scenario, based on a naïve and one-sided appeal to the literature.

Water availability and water shortages

With respect to water supplies and water availability, the Review's information is based mainly on Arnell's studies which indicate that although aggregate populations under water stress through the 2080s – the period considered – may decline, people in some regions could have greater water shortages, while others may have too much water during the rainy season which could lead to both flooding and water shortages during other seasons.[67] But the magnitude of these adverse outcomes is exaggerated since Arnell's papers ignore even the adaptation possible with existing technologies, let alone possibilities from new and improved technologies.[68] No account is taken of the fact that human beings have had a long, and mainly successful, history of combating floods as well as dealing with erratic water flows through a variety of supply and demand side adaptations.[69]

Melting ice sheets

The Review's comments concerning Greenland ice melt are similarly slanted. The text repeatedly emphasizes 'significant melting and an acceleration of ice flows near the coast'[70] and hammers the possibility of 'irreversible' melting of the Greenland ice sheet.[71] Yet, of the four papers relied on, two, based on satellite altimetry, show a slight net gain in the mass of the Greenland ice sheet (over 1992–2002 and 1992–2003), since although the ice margins of Greenland are shrinking, ice is building up inland due to higher snowfall.[72] A third paper, using data from 1996 to 2005, indicates a net loss of ice mass.[73] The fourth study, which uses meteorological models to estimate the overall mass balance of the ice sheet, finds no significant trend from 1961 to 2003.[74] None of these data has been gathered for a sufficiently long period to enable us to discern whether they constitute short-term fluctuations or long-term trends, let alone for us to identify their causes. We note, however, that papers based on longer data series have found that the temperature around the Greenland coast, while it may have risen just in the last few years, is still lower than it was around 1940,[75] and little changed from the very first instrumental measurements in the 1780s.[76]

The Review also fails to mention that temperatures in the Arctic as a whole are only as warm now as they were in the 1930s,[77] or that the much larger Antarctic ice sheet is growing.[78] A continual build-up of snow and ice on the continent will have a tendency to lower mean global sea level.

General health impacts

The estimates presented in the Review for the present day health impacts of climate change and increases in such impacts through 2030 due to a 1 degree C increase in temperature[79] can be traced directly, or indirectly through Patz *et al.* (2005), to McMichael *et al.* (2004).

Evidence of bias can be seen in McMichael's explanation of his method:

> ...climate change occurs against a background of substantial natural climate variability, and its health effects are confounded by simultaneous changes in many other influences on population health...Empirical observation of the health consequences of long-term climate change, followed by formulation, testing and then modification of hypotheses would therefore require long timeseries (probably several decades) of careful monitoring. *While this process may accord with the canons of empirical science, it would not provide the timely information needed to inform current policy decisions on GHG emission abatement*, so as to offset possible health consequences in the future. *Nor would it allow early implementation of policies for adaptation to climate changes.*[80]

In other words, the estimates in this paper are based not on robust science but on a desire to be policy-relevant. The unquestioning use of the McMichael, Patz and WHO studies that have explicit policy concerns is further evidence of partiality and bias.

Malaria and dengue fever

Most of the Review's disease projections are based on Tanser *et al.* (2003), van Lieshout *et al.* (2004) and Hales (2002). Importantly, none of these authors takes account of future changes in technology and increases in adaptive capacities of developing nations as they become richer.[81] Van Lieshout *et al.*, for instance, factor in adaptive capacity as it was in 1990 but they do not allow for improvements in adaptive capacity that can be expected to occur between 1990 and 2085.[82] Notably, Tol and Dowlatabadi (2001) estimate that malaria is functionally eliminated in a society once annual per capita income reaches \$3,100, which is substantially below the average that has been projected in the future for today's developing countries under the poorest (A2) scenario.[83] This is consistent with the basic fact that techniques to eradicate these diseases have been available for decades, so that they are now diseases of poverty, not of climate or climate change.[84]

Extreme weather

In his earlier response to critics in this journal,[85] Sir Nicholas Stern stated that many uncertainties had been resolved in favour of alarm, but that 'one remaining controversy' existed about 'attribution of current weather events to human-induced climate change'. He was wrong on both counts, since while significant uncertainty remains in many areas of climate science, it is very broadly agreed that specific weather events cannot be ascribed to global climate changes, let alone to their hypothesised human-induced component. His response, however, gave the opposite impression by selective citation and claiming, without evidence, that 'The world has been experiencing more extreme weather events.'[86] The latter statement is vague (no base period was stated for the comparison), and contradicts the statements in the last IPCC report that there was:

> ...no compelling evidence that the characteristics of tropical and extra-tropical storms have changed...[and that]...Recent analyses of changes in severe local weather (e.g., tornadoes, thunderstorm days, and hail) in a few selected regions do not provide compelling evidence to suggest long-term changes. In general, trends in severe weather events are notoriously difficult to detect because of their relatively rare occurrence and large spatial variability.[87]

Several studies since the last IPCC report have re-confirmed these statements. For example, to evaluate projections of increased floods and droughts as a result of AGW, Svensson *et al.* (2005) examined river flow data from the Global Runoff Data Centre in Koblenz, Germany with individual record lengths from stations of between 44 to 100 years.[88] The results of this research showed no general pattern of increasing or decreasing numbers or magnitudes of floods. Andreadis and Lettenmaier (2006) examined trends in drought over the continental United States for the period 1925 to 2003 and found that 'droughts have, for the most part, become shorter, less frequent, less severe, and cover a smaller portion of the country'.[89] The June, 2003, issue of the scientific journal *Natural*

Hazards was devoted to assessing whether extreme weather can be attributed to AGW. The editors concluded that most studies find no such connection.

Indeed, elementary considerations of meteorology lead to the conclusion that a warmer world would have less extratropical storminess and variability,[90] while the suggestion of Sir John Houghton that storminess would be abetted by increased evaporation and precipitation (considerations that might be more relevant in the tropics) is inconsistent with the observation that there has been no discernible increase in precipitation since the beginning of satellite measurements.[91]

We note in passing that, contrary to virtually all projections, the 2006 hurricane season in the North Atlantic was relatively mild, underscoring the poor knowledge the climatological community has about the processes that drive storms and extreme weather events, and the folly of giving too much credence to longer-term forecasts based on current knowledge even when forecasting tools have been 'trained' intensely using past information.

To sum up, the Review's analysis of the prospective impacts of possible global warming is consistently biased and selective – and heavily tilted towards unwarranted alarm.

3. The issue of professional standards

The scandal of non-disclosure and poor archiving

Given the global impact of the 'hockey stick', referred to earlier, and similar papers based upon the statistical manipulation of proxy temperature data, one might have expected that governments would by now be insisting that due diligence be applied to all papers concerned with AGW. With the importance now attached to climate prediction, researchers should be required to follow the most stringent professional standards of archiving and disclosure, but with commendable exceptions they do not. Poor disclosure, verification, and media reporting in climate prediction are widespread and a scandal.

The volume of data involved in climate research makes verification of climate prediction impossible without the cooperation of the original workers. The 1998 Mann *et al.* 'hockey stick' paper was soon questioned, but so poor is the archiving of its data and computer programmes that it took almost eight years and direct action from the US House of Representatives for its statistical flaws and lack of robustness to be exposed. By refusing to release data or computer programmes, researchers can effectively prevent verification (which, in science, is the normal route to acceptance) and thereby argue that their thesis has not been falsified.

Some climate scientists who receive generous public funding appear to be determined to maintain self-regulation solely through peer review, and they have been supported in this aim by the British Government and the IPCC.

The contemporary global temperature series as used by the IPCC plays as central a role in climatology as the Consumer Price Index plays in national economic research. The Review shows it as Figure 1.3. Yet it is not produced by a proper statistical agency working under transparent and rigorous protocols. Instead, it is produced by a small, secretive group of researchers at the Climatic Research Unit (CRU) at the University of East Anglia, an organization closely affiliated with the Hadley Centre. The CRU has an explicit policy of refusing to allow external examination of how they produce their global temperature series. In response to a request to examine the underlying data and methods, Dr Phil Jones of the CRU stated: 'Why should I make the data available to you, when your aim is to try and find something wrong with it?' Since scepticism and efforts to falsify hypotheses are fundamental elements of scientific method, we find this statement remarkable. The request came from Australian researcher Warwick Hughes, who wished to examine possible Urban Heat Island (UHI) effects and other bias in the CRU instrumental temperature series. Dr Jones repeated his statement to German climatologist Prof. Hans von Storch,[92] who, in a presentation to the US National Academy of Sciences on March 2, 2006, made clear his astonishment and contempt towards this attitude.

This is by no means an isolated instance. It would be unimaginable for national statistical agencies to take a secretive position regarding the national accounts and price index data they prepare, yet the same situation is regarded as perfectly acceptable within climate science.

In a *Wall Street Journal* interview,[93] asked why he would not cooperate with researchers attempting to replicate his 'hockey stick' diagram, Mann said that he would not be 'intimidated' into releasing his computer programme. When US Congressman Barton later asked for this programme he replied, 'It also bears emphasis that my computer program is a private piece of intellectual property.'[94] This episode triggered a chorus of indignation from climate prediction scientists – not at Mann's attempt to block verification of his publicly-funded paper, but at Congressman Barton's request![95] This, however, raises the question as to whether potentially costly public policies should be based, even in part, on private pieces of intellectual property that, moreover, have not been thoroughly evaluated and replicated.

Full disclosure of all data, statistical techniques and computer code should be a requirement for science used in climate policy formulation, and the Review should have rejected any advice, or publications, for which such disclosure has not been made. The Review should also have advised the UK government to require that full disclosure be made for any future climate science advice that it receives, in line with the recommendations of both the NRC and Wegman panels, and so that the scientific process can function unimpeded by secrecy. The presently permitted secrecy is not only inconsistent with the process of science, but also retards scientific understanding and slows the search for rational policies to address climate change.

Inadequacies of peer review

Policymakers place far too much confidence in the peer review system used by journals, because they misunderstand its purpose and the process. 'Throughout history, most scientists published their views without formal review and peers published their criticisms openly.'[96]

The peer review system was developed comparatively recently by editors of publications to maintain the quality of their journals. But while peer review aims to ensure that papers are well-framed and advance hypotheses worthy of consideration by the scientific community, it was never intended to provide a guarantee that hypotheses or recommendations advanced in papers were correct or unchallengeable. In particular, it is no safeguard against dubious assumptions, arguments and conclusions if the peers are largely drawn from the same restricted professional milieu as the authors. Moreover, as the examples above show, peer review does not even ensure that data and methods are open to scrutiny or that results are reproducible.

Bias in science is not usually intentional or even conscious, but it is especially prone to occur when consensus views are sought or expressed. Prof. von Storch, who is review editor of the 'Regional Climate Projections' chapter of the IPCC's forthcoming assessment report, recently warned[97] that 'exaggerat[ed] claims pass the internal quality checks of science relatively easily, whereas more reasoned and scientifically accurate claims find an unwelcome audience among scientists'. He went on to argue that 'The practice of scientists exaggerating threatening perspectives of anthropogenic climate change and its implications serves not only the purpose of supporting a policy perceived as 'good' but also personal agendas of career and public visibility'.

A recent example of how easily flawed papers supporting the alarmist view can pass peer review is that of Chuine et al.,[98] who claimed that they could derive the summer temperature in Burgundy for any year back to 1370 from the dates of grape harvests. The paper concluded that 2003 was the warmest year since 1370, a dramatic conclusion which helped it gain acceptance in *Nature* and wide attention for the authors. A statistician, Douglas J. Keenan,[99] engaged in a long effort to obtain the authors' data, and eventually was able to show that while the Chuine *et al.* model treated moderate summers well, it was without statistical merit for estimating exceptionally warm years. The problem for the use of this type of science in the public arena is that far more lay people will have seen or heard media reports of the original paper than hear of its rebuttal. Keenan says on his web page (our emphasis), 'What is important here is not the truth or falsity of the assertion of Chuine et al. about Burgundy temperatures. Rather, what is important is that *a paper on what is arguably the world's most important scientific topic [global warming] was published in the world's most prestigious scientific journal with essentially no checking of the work prior to publication.'*

Few papers in climate science are independently verified, often because of the difficulties in getting the original data as reported above. When the few papers that are critical of the consensus view are published they are often met with a chorus of criticism for their lack of, or inferior, peer review, which stifles discussion of the disputed issues. The dispute over the Mann *et al.* paper is an object lesson both as to why those papers based upon large data sets and advanced statistical techniques should be verified, and why peer review alone is inadequate. From what has now been disclosed, and thoroughly investigated, we know that the criticisms of the Mann *et al.* paper that were rebuffed by many, including the British government, by repeated reference to peer review, were accurate. Those including the British government who continued to defend the 'hockey stick' work because it had been peer reviewed simply missed the point. Based on this experience, the IPCC peer review process provides no safeguard against dubious assumptions, arguments and conclusions. This is particularly so as, over time, dissenting panellists[100] have withdrawn from the IPCC process, thereby reducing it to a restricted professional milieu within which close colleagues frequently review their own work or that of close colleagues.

4. Conclusion

We conclude that the Stern Review is biased and alarmist in its reading of the science. In particular, it displays:

- a failure to acknowledge the scope and scale of the knowledge gaps and uncertainties in climate science

- credulous acceptance of hypothetical, model-based explanations of the causality of climate phenomena

- massive overestimation of climate impacts through an implausible population scenario and one-sided treatment of the impacts literature, including reliance on agenda-driven advocacy documents

- lack of due diligence in evaluating many pivotal research studies despite the scandalous lack of disclosure of data and methods in these studies
- lack of concern for the defects and inadequacies of the peer review process as a guarantor of quality or truth.

These and other related problems arise because the Review has relied for advice almost exclusively on a small number of people and organizations that have a long history of unbalanced alarmism on the global warming issue. Most of the research cited by the Review does not, on inspection, make a convincing case that greenhouse warming constitutes a major threat that justifies an immediate and radical policy response. Contrary research is consistently ignored, as are basic observational facts showing that alarm is unwarranted.

The Review fails to present an accurate picture of scientific understanding of climate change issues, and will reinforce ill-informed alarm about climate change among the general public, the bureaucracy and the body politic. HM Government will need to look elsewhere for a balanced, impartial and authoritative review of the current climate change debate.

Annex: The Stern Review's mishandling of basic observational data

The Review's presentations of data on the key parameters of the greenhouse equation – emissions, concentrations, and forcing – are inconsistent and unreliable. For example, the Review puts the worst possible face on emission trends:

> Emissions of CO_2, which accounts for the largest share of greenhouse gases, grew at an average annual rate of around 2½% between 1950 and 2000.[101]

The statement is only true if one ignores all natural emissions, which the Review does persistently and carelessly.[102] At the same time, however, the statement obscures the more important point that the rate of emissions growth fell throughout the period, as Figure 1 shows.[103]

The Review's handling of current CO_2 equivalent (CO_2e) levels is incompetent. Its first mention of the concept is the following:

> The warming effect due to all (Kyoto) greenhouse gases emitted by human activities is now equivalent to around 430 ppm of carbon dioxide.[104]

This is wrong. If the current CO_2e level is 430 ppm, then the warming effect due to all (Kyoto) greenhouse gases emitted by human activities is actually equivalent to only 150 ppm of carbon dioxide, since 280 ppm of carbon dioxide was already in the atmosphere in the pre-industrial era.[105]

Note, however, that even with this correction, the statement still glides too easily over the difference between emissions from human activities and concentrations. CO_2e levels are concentrations, and concentrations do not simply

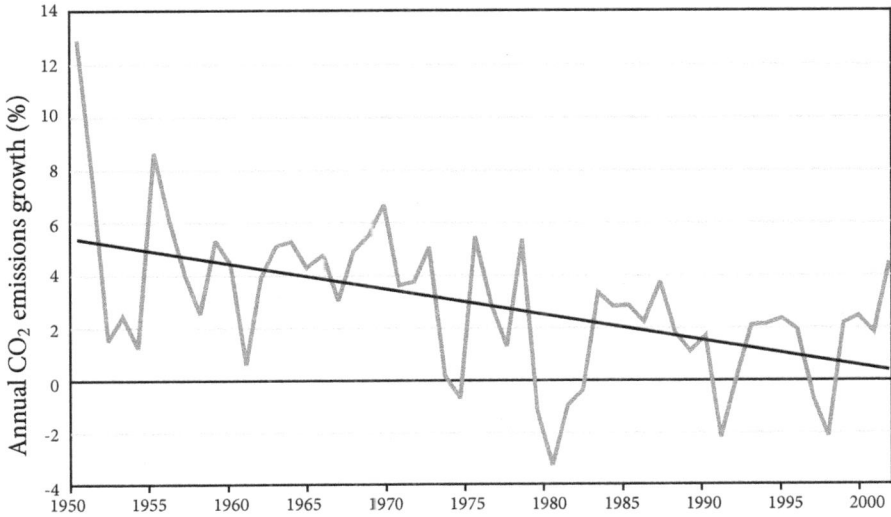

Figure 1: Annual growth of anthropogenic CO_2 emissions, 1950–2003

increase by the amount of emissions from human activities. In fact, most GHGs emitted by human activities have been either reabsorbed by the biosphere (this is the case for about 60% of total man-made CO_2 emissions to date) or destroyed by chemical reactions in the atmosphere (as is the case for methane, nitrous oxide, etc.).

The Review also quotes inconsistent figures for CO_2e levels. The OXONIA Lecture gives 425 ppm. The Review generally quotes 430 ppm, but this excludes CFCs solely because they are regulated by the Montreal Protocol rather than the Kyoto Protocol. Including the CFCs, the Review states the figure would be 445 ppm.[106] Yet Box 8.2 on page 202 gives a current level of 450 ppm for Kyoto gases only, implying a total, including CFCs, of 465 ppm. The true figure may be higher still, as recent papers suggest that the radiative forcing of methane has been underestimated.[107]

The Review says that 'The rate of annual increase in greenhouse gas levels is variable year-on-year, but is increasing.'[108] 8This is not true, as examination of the data behind the graph presented to back this statement shows.[109] There has been a clear fall in the rate of increase of total GHGs (including CFCs) since the mid-1980s. The fall would have been clearer still if the graph had been on a logarithmic scale, which it should have been in order to reflect the true increase in forcing.

This skews the treatment of *likely future increases in GHGs* towards a worst-case scenario. Page 176 of the Review says, 'Emissions are rising. But suppose they continue to add to GHG concentrations by only 3ppm a year...' This implies both that 3 ppm is the current rate, and that it is a reasonable minimum rate for the future. Neither proposition is true. Other parts of the Review give the current rate of increase at 'about 2.7ppm CO_2e per year',[110] 'roughly 2.5 ppm every year',[111] and 'around 2.3 ppm per year'.[112] In fact, over the last 10 years it only averaged 2.2 ppm, and the trend seems downwards, with 1.7 ppm the likely outcome for 2006.[113] Taking 3 ppm as a minimum future value is thus excessively pessimistic. Yet the Review goes even further when it proposes that 'In a plausible 'business as usual' scenario, they [concentrations] will reach 550ppm CO_2e by 2035.'[114] As this is based on the Review's assumption that current concentrations are only 430 ppm, it requires an increase of 120 ppm in 30 years, an average of 4 ppm per year. This is unrealistic: it is double the current rate and higher even than the record average level in the peak years of 1976–1988.

The excessive projections derive from ignoring hard data on concentration trends, and instead using carbon cycle models to predict concentrations from projected emissions. A good test of the reliability of this approach is to compare model predictions for methane with actual observations. Since methane has a shorter atmospheric lifetime than CO_2, it shows the reliability of modelling more quickly. As Figure 2 illustrates, modelling concentrations from emissions is still a very inexact science.[115]

The real, observed concentration of methane has not increased for the last 7 years, contrary to all IPCC modelling and scenarios.[116] While the first chapter of the Review mentions methane more than 20 times and repeatedly emphasises the possibilities for massive escape of the gas from thawing permafrost or ocean hydrates, it fails to observe this important change in atmospheric forcing, let alone discuss possible explanations.[117]

The Review correctly states that 'the warming effect of carbon dioxide rises approximately logarithmically with its concentration in the atmosphere', but then immediately adds, wrongly, that *methane and nitrous oxide concentrations have a linear relationship to radiative forcing*.[118] In fact, forcing declines with concentration increments, as shown in Figure 3 for methane using the IPCC formula.[119]

Leaving aside the Review's mistake in describing CO_2e levels, all its misstatements of data on emissions, concentrations and forcing follow a consistent pattern. In each case, total change to date – which has been substantial, but harmless – is minimised. By contrast, present and likely future rates of change – which are presented as having dire consequences – are exaggerated. The Review's data distortions are systematically biased towards alarm.

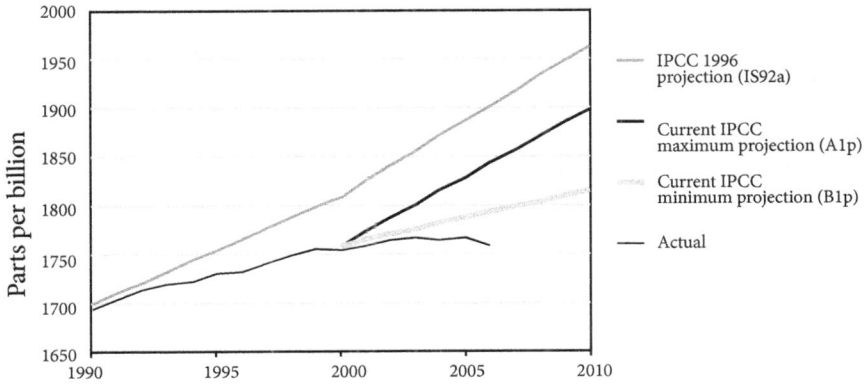

Figure 2: Atmospheric abundance of methane

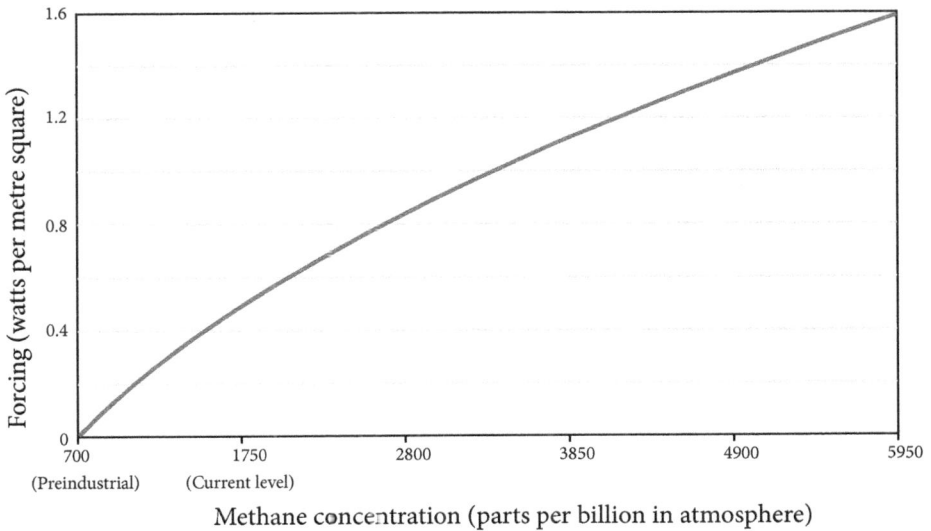

Methane concentration (parts per billion in atmosphere)

Figure 3: The radiative forcing of methane.

IPCC Third Assessment Report formula, relative to pre-industrial level.

Part II: Economic aspects

Ian Byatt, Ian Castles, Indur M. Goklany, David Henderson, Nigel Lawson, Ross McKitrick, Julian Morris, Alan Peacock, Colin Robinson and Robert Skidelsky

Introduction

The starting point of the Stern Review is that 'The scientific evidence is now overwhelming: climate change is a serious global threat...' For reasons that are set out in Part I above, we believe that this assertion is not correct, and that the Review's treatment of scientific issues is open to serious question. Here we go on to question its treatment of economic issues.

This is no straightforward task, because of the lack of clarity which characterises much of the Review's analysis. This has been noted by others: in the article of theirs that follows, and which likewise comments on the Review, Richard Tol and Gary Yohe make the point that 'It is impossible for a reader to understand precisely what is in the calculations that underlie' the Review; and in the same vein, William Nordhaus has written that 'It is virtually impossible for mortals outside the group that did the modeling to understand the detailed results of the Review'. In an after-the-event attempt to clarify matters, a Postscript to the Review, accompanied by a Technical Annex on modelling issues, was published just before this article went to press. But much remains unclear, placing an undue burden on readers to excavate the actual structure of the Review's argument.

Our treatment below falls under six headings. We start in Section 1 by considering the Review's valuation of the possible *impacts* of global warming. Here our point of departure is Section 2 of Part I above, where our scientific colleagues have assessed what the Stern Review says about prospective biophysical impacts. With their conclusions as a basis, we move on to consider, and to put in question, the figures that the Review derives for the prospective costs of these various impacts, and hence for the benefits that would supposedly flow from policies to reduce emissions.

From the projected benefits of mitigation, we turn in Section 2 to consider the prospective costs involved. We think that the Stern Review has understated these, probably by a wide margin. The combination of projected benefits that are pitched too high and projected costs that are pitched too low has led to a seriously unbalanced presentation of policy alternatives.

In Section 3, we consider the central issue of discounting the future. Here again we give reasons to question the Review's treatment. Critical issues are not fully explored, the bias towards immediate and far-reaching actions to reduce emissions is reinforced, and the risks and problems that would arise from following the Review's prescriptions for policy are not faced.

Under all these headings, a recurrent theme is that the Review positions itself well outside the mainstream of published economic writings on these subjects: in relation to the professional debate, it appears as an outlier.

In Section 4, we consider the choice of policy instruments in the context of climate change, and comment on the treatment of these issues in the Review. Section 5 deals with further major omissions from the Review – issues, and contributions to the subject, which the document fails to consider. Some of the points that we make here form a counterpart and extension of the argument in Section 3 of Part I above: we draw attention, as our scientific colleagues have done, to an established and officially approved process of inquiry which is not professionally up to the mark. Section 6 summarises our conclusions.

The Review shows serious weaknesses in its treatment and presentation of basic data. The Annex to Part I comments on one aspect of this failing, namely, the mishandling of basic observational data relating to climate change and the factors that bear on it. Here we present a counterpart annex of a similar kind. It deals with the Review's faulty handling of sources which are themselves flawed. The sources in question are the emissions scenarios which form the starting point for the Third Assessment Report of the Intergovernmental Panel on Climate Change (IPCC).

1. Valuing possible impacts

Biased alarmism

The Review presents a dark and dramatic picture of the possible consequences of global warming. The main message is conveyed in the following excerpts, already much quoted by commentators, from the Summary of Conclusions (p. vi):

> Using the results from formal economic models, the Review estimates that if we don't act, the overall costs and risks of climate change will be equivalent to losing at least 5% of global GDP each year, now and forever. If a wider range of risks and impacts is taken into account, the estimates of damage could rise to 20% of GDP or more.

> Our actions now and over the coming decades could create risks of major disruption to economic and social activity, on a scale similar to those associated with the great wars and the economic depression of the first half of the 20th century.

Such conjectures – for they are no more than that – are built up in two stages: first, the possible biophysical impacts over time are listed and reviewed; and second, values are attached to these in order to derive measures of their possible effect on human well-being, as in the numbers just quoted.

For both stages, the results presented in the Review refer to possible future developments *over a period of two centuries or more*. This fact alone gives grounds for caution. Both theory and past experience suggest that 'results from formal economic models' are a highly unreliable guide to what may happen so far ahead, while similar doubts can be entertained about the scientific inputs which in this instance form the point of departure for the models.

The Review's treatment of projected biophysical impacts of global warming has been analysed above in Part I. Drawing on a wide range of published sources, the authors review the evidence relating to hunger and agricultural productivity; ecosystems and extinction risks; water availability and shortages; melting ice sheets; general health impacts; malaria and dengue fever; and extreme weather events. They demonstrate that 'the Review's analysis of the prospective impacts of possible global warming is consistently biased and selective – and heavily tilted towards unwarranted alarm'. This conclusion bears on the dramatic claims that the Review makes about the prospective *values* to be attached to these impacts, which consequently appear as greatly overstated.

The arguments set out in Part I are not confined to purely biophysical outcomes: the two aspects, scientific and economic, are partly overlapping. The authors rightly note that the studies which the Review relies on take inadequate account, or no account at all, of the fact that people, enterprises and institutions generally can be expected to adapt their conduct, and the forms which their investment for the future takes, in response to both the experience and the prospect of global warming: now as in the past, they would not just be passive and helpless spectators of climate change. The Review also downplays the possibilities for adaptation arising from future technical progress, the more so since (1) the emergence or prospect of global warming as a problem would increase the incentive for such progress to be directed towards ways of adapting to it, and (2) the time horizon under review is so extended. To disregard or underplay both adaptive behaviour and technical progress is not an acceptable way of defining 'business as usual'.[120]

In weighing the prospects for adaptation, the Review presents a picture of the prospects for developing countries in particular which is in part misleading. It emphasises that adaptation is harder in countries with low levels of GDP per head. But it takes no account of the fact that, in the scenarios that it quotes from the Special Report on Emissions Scenarios (SRES) which point towards high levels of global warming, the projections of GDP per head yield the result that developing countries in general are no longer poor by absolute standards by the time that seriously damaging impacts from warming are seen as emerging.[121]

Given such projections of their long-term growth, and the possibilities for re-sourceful action that this increasing prosperity would help to open up, it is not reasonable to portray the developing countries over the longer term as hapless victims of change.[122] In this connection, a point worth noting is that in indus-trial economies climate has little effect on economic activity. Most of the world's economic activity today takes place indoors: generally speaking, the outputs of both manufacturing and services are unaffected by outdoor conditions. Again, resource extraction also carries on under widely varying climatic conditions, since its location is determined by the resource deposit. In developed coun-tries, only agriculture and forestry can realistically be considered vulnerable to climate change, while for the mid-latitudes, available projections suggest that warming may in fact be beneficial. Only in those lower-latitude countries where the primary sector occupies a large fraction of GDP, and in particular poor tropi-cal countries, does warming as such appear as a possibly significant direct threat to the conduct of economic activity. While the Review rather grudgingly admits that this is the case, it does not make the point that on generally accepted pro-jections of future growth in GDP per head, which it does not put in doubt, the share of these vulnerable sectors can be expected to decline to a relatively low level.

Model-based speculations

The Review spends considerable time discussing Integrated Assessment Model results from the economics literature. Figure 6.2 in the Review shows, for what they are worth, long-term projections of the economic costs associated with global warming scenarios from zero to about 6 degrees C, as computed by some of the most prominent authors in the field. As noted in Part I, the situation as currently understood points to modest warming trends at most. Up to the 2C level, the model simulations as presented suggest zero or negative expected net costs from climate change. Beyond 2C, two of the three models show moder-ate global costs of less than 2 per cent of GDP; and furthermore, they indicate that the costs level off quickly, even out to a 6C warming scenario. Only the Nordhaus and Boyer analysis appears to suggest increasing marginal costs. But this property of their model arises from the same kind of methodological de-parture that features in the Stern Review – namely, adding in very speculative non-economic costs with little empirical guidance. The Review acknowledges (p. 152) that, in the Nordhaus–Boyer model, the conventional direct economic costs are only one-tenth of those shown in Figure 6.2, the remainder being spec-ulative 'multiplier effects' operating through investment; and even then, as the Review notes, policy analysis based on the Nordhaus model does not support aggressive emission reductions (see Section 4 below).

Thus, looking at the economics information presented in the Review itself, neither the Integrated Assessment Models nor the IPCC scenarios provide a credible basis for expecting dramatic economic damages from global warming. This can fairly be described as the consensus position in the economics literature. Yet the Review summarily sets it aside. Instead, beginning on p. 149, it appeals to new insights of its own:

> Existing estimates of the monetary cost of climate change, although very useful, leave many questions unanswered and omit potentially very important impacts. Taking omitted impacts into account will increase cost estimates, and probably strongly.

The Review then positions itself as an outlier by referring to two working papers (cited as Watkiss 2005; Warren et al. 2006) as the basis for dramatically ramping up estimates of damages due to extreme weather, 'social and political instability', and 'knock-on effects'. Of these three, the Review's treatment of extreme weather is questioned in Part I; some experts in the field are more severe in their criticism.[123] The latter two influences are not at all clearly defined: the reader can consult the Review (pp. 151–152) to try to make headway. Later they are grouped into 'nonmarket impact' and 'risk of catastrophe' effects, though with little further definition provided. According to the Review, they account for some 80–90 per cent of the projected damages due to global warming, and yet everybody else seems to have missed them.

These speculations have two effects: they bump up the projected climate warming outcomes (see Box 6.1, p. 154), and they add (massively) to the expected costs in the model runs from the PAGE 2002 model on which the Review places heavy reliance. Table 6.1 (p. 163) shows that from the PAGE model one obtains a span of economic costs from the business-as-usual climate change simulation, 90 per cent of which fall between 0.3 and 7.5 per cent (of total current consumption), depending on whether the regular model or the 'high climate' amplified version is used. This is already high compared to the mainstream distribution, but the Review is only getting started – and the later Technical Annex serves to amplify the effects even further. Once the vaguely-defined 'non-market impacts' and 'risk of catastrophe' categories are added in, the economic costs come to span 2.2 to 32.6 per cent of total consumption. These additional elements thus amplify the impacts by factors ranging from 4.3 to nine.

To sum up: from 80 to 90 per cent of the impacts of climate change estimated by the Review comprise novel and conjectural cost categories that are not used by the large majority of experts who have studied this issue up to now; that rely on arbitrary amplifications to regular climate model processes; and which have not received proper critical attention in the peer-reviewed economics literature.

This is not an acceptable procedure. It might have been defensible to include such speculative extensions in a second round of estimates, after having first presented results based on the existing published assessments of economic damages as recognised in the economics literature to date. But to present these novel, outlier concepts as the central results of the Review betrays a lack of balance.

From projected physical impacts to the figures quoted above, of damages which amount to 'at least 5% of global GDP' and possibly '20% or more', 'now and forever', there is in fact a sequence of argument by which, to take over a phrase from Nordhaus, 'a few more gloomy ingredients are stirred in'. It is via this poorly explained and highly coloured process of accretion that the Review finally derives its startlingly high conjectural figures for the damages that it sees as resulting from the continued pursuit of what it misleadingly portrays as 'business as usual'. Since the treatment of projected damages and disasters is so flawed, these final results cannot be taken at face value: they reflect a bias towards speculative alarmism.

Behind the high damage estimates are emissions estimates that seem themselves to be pessimistic as regards economic pressures for conservation. As relative costs and prices change, new technologies will be adopted because they are profitable: energy saving is an obvious example. As the Review notes, there has been a very big improvement in the fuel efficiency of electricity generation over time; and indeed there is a long history in most developed countries of decline in the energy intensity of GDP. Experience after the 'oil shocks' of the 1970s and early 1980s demonstrated the responsiveness of energy consumption to energy price increases. The elasticity of energy demand with respect to price is low in the short run because the presence of an inherited stock of energy-using equipment limits the extent of switching and conservation (Robinson, 1988). But the Review takes a very long view, and in the medium and long terms, the elasticity is much higher as the stock changes in response to changes in the price of energy relative to other goods and the relative prices of different energy sources. World energy consumption, which had increased at a compound rate of over 5 per cent per annum between 1950 and 1973, continued to rise for a few years after the first oil shock in 1973–74 but then stopped increasing in the first half of the 1980s (BP, 2006). Recent increases in oil and other energy prices are also likely, after a time lag, to bring about a similar response.

In other words, a realistic 'business as usual' (BAU) scenario is itself likely to contain significant energy-saving technological advances that will reduce carbon emissions. This is a further reason why the damage resulting from carbon emissions under BAU may well be significantly less than the Review projects.

2. The estimated costs of mitigation

Downward bias

Just as the Review exaggerates damages, so it produces surprisingly low estimates of the costs of abatement. Since it is not clear what the extent of carbon reductions would be under BAU, trying to estimate the costs of further reductions beyond this unknown base becomes a highly speculative exercise. There is a long history of 'appraisal optimism' in attempts to estimate the costs of energy sources which would not come to market without some form of government subsidisation or other form of promotion. The massive under-estimation of future costs in Britain's successive government-promoted nuclear power programmes from the 1950s onwards is the example nearest to home (Helm, 2003), but there has been a general tendency to underestimate the costs of energy sources that might replace fossil fuels.

One reason why mitigation costs appear low relative to damage costs is because the Review applies its own relatively low rate of interest in discounting projected future costs and benefits: we consider this aspect in Section 3 below. However, other influences also enter into the result.

In chapter 9 of the Review, an analysis of technologies that would help reduce carbon emissions, and their possible costs, results in mitigation cost estimates of −1 per cent to +3.5 per cent of GDP by 2050, with an average of around 1 per cent. The list of carbon-reducing technologies is one about which there is some consensus among energy specialists (though that is not to say that it will turn out correct, since technological forecasting has a very poor record). But there is considerable doubt about the cost of forcing the adoption of such technologies over and above what would occur without such forcing.

Chapter 9 gives some indication of the uncertainty surrounding its mitigation cost estimates. These depend to a large extent on the work of Dennis Anderson, who has drawn on a number of studies, often by official bodies. Anderson puts the average cost of carbon abatement in 2005 at £225/tonC; but this figure is projected to fall, as a result of incentives, innovation and technical progress to £145 by 2015, £85 by 2020 and £60 by 2050.[124] The Review (p. 231, Figure 9.5) translates the £225/tonC into $100/CO_2$, which exceeds Stern's own estimate, of ($85/tonCO_2e$), which itself is high in comparison with other studies.

The Review estimates (p. 233) a technology uncertainty of 4.3% of world GDP, far bigger than the energy price uncertainty of 2.2% (both by 2050). When writing about carbon capture, Anderson says: 'even in the near to medium term, the uncertainties are very large.' Two examples that he gives are:

> [carbon capture and storage] (CCS) is expected to play a crucial role...the range of cost estimates will be narrow when CCS technologies have been

demonstrated but, until this occurs, the estimates remain speculative.

> The costs of carbon abatement are expected to decline by half over the next 20 years, and then by a third further by 2050. But the longer term estimates of shifting to a low-carbon energy system span a very broad range as indicated... and may even be broader than estimated here.

Anderson also makes the important point that in optimisation models, the results change kaleidoscopally with small changes in relative cost assumptions.

This emphasis on uncertainty is appropriate. However, here as in other parts of the Review, the qualifications made in the body of the document receive little attention when conclusions are drawn. By the end of chapter 9, it is concluded that mitigation costs are likely to be 1±2.5 per cent of annual GDP – which seems a very small range compared with the highly speculative nature of the estimates; and the Executive Summary (p. xiii) removes all reference to a range of uncertainty, giving the 'upper bound' for the annual cost of emission reductions as 1 per cent of GDP.

Chapter 10 of the Review goes on to discuss mitigation cost estimates derived from macro-economic modelling exercises, with supporting discussion in Chapter 12. The Chapter 10 estimates are generally consistent with those in Chapter 9, concluding that estimates of mitigation costs in 2050 centre on 1 per cent of GDP, with a range of –2 to +5 per cent of GDP. While reference is made to the work of many mainstream analysts, heavy reliance is placed on a single meta analysis (cited in the Review as Barker et al. 2006).

The Review's Table 10.1 summarises the span of surveyed cost estimates for mitigation policy packages adequate to cap atmospheric CO_2 at 450 ppm. The basic cost is 3.4 per cent of global output. This is then whittled away by invoking a number of assumptions, until the 3.4 per cent cost of mitigation becomes a 3.9 per cent economic gain – a very large free lunch.

The revenue-cycling aspect

The largest single cost reduction (1.9 per cent of global output) is arrived at by assuming 'active revenue recycling'. Revenue recycling refers to the fact that some emission pricing policies (taxes, auctioned permits) generate revenue for the government, and this added revenue could be used to finance a cut in other tax rates. In order to model the effects of revenue recycling, however, the cost estimation must be done in a model that includes a full treatment of the tax system. Table 10.1 applies a large cost reduction to all the models surveyed, but notes in a footnote (fn. 4, p. 243) that revenue recycling was a feature only of one model examined.

There is a problem with arbitrarily deducting the benefits of revenue recycling from mitigation cost estimates computed in models without a full treatment of the tax system. The problem is that adding in a proper treatment of the system increases the estimated mitigation costs through 'tax interaction' effects. In studies that have examined this issue, tax interaction costs are typically as large as or larger than revenue recycling effects, so that it is invalid to assume that revenue recycling can be counted against the cost estimates shown in Table 10.1.

Numerous well known studies, not mentioned in the Review, have concluded that in order to measure the recycling benefit in a theoretically sound way, tax interaction costs must also be modelled (e.g. Bovenberg and de Mooij 1994; Fullerton 1997). Tax interaction effects arise from consideration of the conventional deadweight costs of taxation. A tax drives a wedge between the buyer price and the seller price, destroying more consumer and producer surplus than the tax revenue created. This 'excess burden' is a function of the tax rates and the parameters of demand and supply in the market affected. The cross-price effects of introducing a new tax in one market will affect the excess burden in other markets; and in specific circumstances they will increase that burden in related markets. Empirical examination by economists (e.g. Parry 1995; Bovenberg and Goulder 1996) has shown that emissions taxes will typically interact with factor markets (labour and capital) in such a way as to increase the preexisting excess burdens, generating positive costs due to tax interaction effects. These effects grow in step with – and indeed slightly faster than – the potential benefits from revenue recycling. This result confirms an early theoretical argument by Agnar Sandmo (1975). Rather than this item bringing a net reduction to modelled costs, therefore, it should be viewed as tending to increase them.

There is also a time dimension here. Insofar as carbon taxes are progressively effective in reducing emissions, their revenue yield will fall accordingly, and this will limit the possibilities for revenue recycling. The Review relies on a model without a tax system and hence does not take into account the changing public finance aspects over time.

The domain of conjecture

Besides the questionable gains from 'recycling', Table 10.1 in the Review also allows for arbitrary, free lunch-style 'induced technology' benefits, and for gains due to ancillary reductions in conventional pollution. These influences, which are far from well defined, bring down the projected costs by a further 0.5 per cent of global GDP. They are elaborated in Chapter 12, where, however, the cited literature is notably heavy on unpublished NGO discussion papers and industry promotional brochures. Another significant effect (0.4 per cent) comes under the heading of 'climate benefit', which however remains undefined.

This whole analysis largely relates to a conjectural future: little attention is given to actual past experience. Measures and programmes to reduce CO_2 emissions have been in place for some years, in Britain and elsewhere. The costs and effects of these could have been reviewed, with an eye to the evidence they provide and the lessons to be drawn from them. Such a survey, impartially conducted, would have been a useful contribution to knowledge. Four of us (Byatt, Henderson, Peacock and Robinson) made this point in submitting evidence at the outset of the Review: we suggested that the costs of British mitigation policies, current and prospective, should be identified and documented. This suggestion was not acted on: here as elsewhere, the Review appears as more focused on hypothetical futures than on the evidence and experience of the past.

Much depends on the kinds of measures that are adopted by way of mitigation. Insofar as reliance is placed on regulatory instruments, costs are likely to be appreciably higher. (Here again there may already be useful lessons to be drawn from actual experience to date). Concerned about 'market imperfections', the Review questions the capacity of market-led technological change to adapt to the climate change 'threat'. On the other hand, it seems remarkably optimistic, in the face of past evidence, about the ability of governments to pick technological 'winners' and bring them successfully into the market.

Weighing costs and benefits

The treatment of costs and benefits in the Stern Review is deeply flawed. First, the Review either overlooks or sets aside important elements of the professional literature in favour of its own views, which read as outliers by comparison. Second, whereas the Review is biased towards technological pessimism when assessing the costs of climate change, it is equally (and inconsistently) biased towards technological optimism concerning largescale mitigation efforts, alternate energy, and so forth. Its treatment of the issues is neither balanced nor credible.

3. Discounting and intergenerational equity

Discounting the future

The comparison of early costs with longer-term benefits is crucial to the conclusion that there is a strong economic case for immediate action on the scale recommended. The Review's conclusions largely derive from the use of social time preference theory, which suggests a discount rate based on (1) pure inter-generational time preference, (2) an assumption as to the future growth of consumption, and (3) a figure for the elasticity of marginal utility with respect to consumption. The numbers chosen by the Review are all open to question and, as the later Technical Annex shows, the results are not robust. What is more, the Review takes no account of the opportunity cost of crowding out other forms of future-directed expenditure.

Welfare economists have treated the issue of allocating consumption across generations using a discount rate that separates into three components, in such a way as to allow the welfare of those now living to be compared with that of future generations, taking into account the fact that because of consumption growth the latter can be expected to be more prosperous. The Review goes over the standard discount rate decomposition, which yields:

$$\rho = \eta \frac{\dot{C}}{C} + \delta$$

where C is consumption per head, $\frac{\dot{C}}{C}$ is its projected rate of change, δ is the pure rate of time preference, η (eta) is the rate of change of marginal utility as consumption increases ($C \times U''/U'$, where U is the utility function) and ρ is the resulting discount rate to be applied to public sector projects. To derive the appropriate social time preference rate, values thus have to be assigned to all three of the parameters involved.

Choosing parameters

The choice of values depends on assessments and evaluations which are inherently open to debate. Differing views can be held about the future growth of consumption per head, and different positions can be taken as to the ethical considerations that bear on the values assigned to the other two parameters. Since the issues here are both inescapable and unsettled, no short cuts are permissible. A serious treatment should be both balanced and transparent; and it should explore, through careful sensitivity analysis, the implications of taking different combinations of values. It is against this background that the treatment in the Review has to be weighed.

For the parameter delta, the Review explicitly adopts a value of 0.1 per cent per annum, which is of course a very low figure. To say this is not to reject it. The choice of a low pure time preference rate, as with other parameter values, could be defended if presented as illustrative and plausible, rather than definitive, and if the reader was shown, through the medium of a sensitivity analysis, the implications of other possible choices.

As to the other two parameters, the Review does not specify the values that it has taken, so that its recommended social time reference rate likewise remains undisclosed. This is not a transparent procedure. Further, the Review *provides no sensitivity analysis*. These twin omissions add up to a serious lapse.[125]

Since the appearance of the Review, some progress has been made in making good these deficiencies. First, it has been revealed that the Review sets the value for eta at unity, and that it takes the growth rate of world consumption per head over the next three centuries to be, respectively, 2.0, 1.8, and 1.3 per cent per annum. (The latter rate is assumed to hold perpetually thereafter).[126] Allowing for pure time preference, this implies discount rates, century by century, of 2.1, 1.9, and 1.4 per cent per annum.

The Review argues that the presence of uncertainty should reduce the discount rate used. However, many would argue that, because our knowledge of future events becomes more uncertain as the time horizon is extended, discount rates should if anything increase rather than diminish with time.

The Review's failure to provide sensitivity analysis has been partially remedied in the later Technical Annex. Different values have been run there, through the PAGE 2002 model, for the pure time discount rate (delta) and for the elasticity of the marginal utility of consumption (eta). However, these variations have been treated separately and not in conjunction, while no complementary sensitivity analysis has been performed with respect to the growth rate of consumption per head. Further, the Annex obscures the discount rate sensitivity analysis by simultaneously increasing the damage function parameter: it offers a wholly implausible set of simulations in which the already-exaggerated damage costs are further amplified. Its procedures are neither thorough nor transparent, and appear designed to persuade the reader that sensitivity analysis leaves intact the Review's alarmist projections.

Despite its limitations, this belated sensitivity analysis yields some illuminating results. First, the pure time preference rate. In Table PA-3 of the Annex, the average monetary cost of what is taken as a 'business as usual' scenario falls by nearly three-quarters, from 5.0 per cent of global GDP to 1.4 per cent, when the Review's preferred rate of 0.1 per cent per annum is replaced by 1.5 per cent, thus raising the recommended discount rate from 2.1 per cent per annum to 3.5 per cent which cannot be viewed as an especially high figure.[127]

Second, in the case of eta, the Annex analyses the result of taking a value of 1.5 rather than 1.0: such a figure would not be inconsistent with the distributional concerns in the Review.[128] Here the effect is to reduce prospective damage (as defined above) from 5.0 per cent of global GDP to 2.9 per cent. In combination with the 0.1 per cent pure time preference rate, this value of 1.5 yields a discount rate of 3.1 per cent per annum.

Unfortunately, the two sensitivities are not combined in the Annex; and we still await a proper sensitivity analysis on all three parameters, possibly in the form of the Monte Carlo analysis used elsewhere in the Review. Nevertheless, the scale of the potential effect on damage projections, as already revealed by this incomplete sensitivity analysis, shows that when different values are assigned very different results emerge, pointing to very different policy conclusions.

Weighing the present against the future

This is not the place to consider the much-debated issue of just how the welfare of those living today is to be weighed and assessed in relation to that of future generations.[129] But it should be noted that the particular combination of values that the Review favours, of 0.1 per cent for delta and unity for eta, and the low rate of discount which goes with them, point to very high rates of saving for the current generation.

This fact is brought out in a paper by Partha Dasgupta commenting on the Stern Review. He notes that 'in a deterministic economy where the social rate of return on investment is, say, 4% a year', building in the above values for delta and eta leads to the conclusion that '*the current generation in that model economy ought to save a full 97.5% of its GDP for the future!*' (italics in the original). The Review briefly alludes (p. 47) to the argument that low values of eta yield implausibly high implied savings rates, but waves away Arrow's well known exposure of the problem by saying that it is not convincing. This is not a serious treatment of the issue.

To prescribe such high rates of current saving appears to give too little weight to the interests of the world's poor today and in the near to medium future. The Review makes much of the need to transfer resources now from developed to developing countries. But this concern with poverty today is not easy to square with the use of such a low discount rate, which *inter alia* implies that the present generation of poor people ought to transfer, via a much higher savings rate than now, a substantially greater part of its income to future generations who will be, on the Review's own assumptions, much wealthier. A way of meeting this objection is to prescribe that the extra burden of reduced consumption and higher savings today should be borne by the rich countries alone; and this seems to be the position that the Review takes. It does not, however, consider how far the imposition of such a considerable extra burden on these countries would be consistent with its surprisingly low estimate of the costs of mitigation.

It is a peculiar feature of the Review that while forecasting that people in the future will be vastly richer than today, it also proposes that the present generation should make substantial new sacrifices on behalf of these more prosperous generations. It is as though, looking back two hundred years (a period comparable to the one the Review purports to cover), we claimed that people living in the early days of industrialisation ought to have made sacrifices on behalf of those living today, even though we are rich beyond the dreams of anyone in those distant times.

The problem of dual standards

The recommendation of the Review is that all future-directed expenditures that are oriented towards reducing future emissions, often if not always with effects that are seen as long term or remote in time, should be evaluated at the real (social time preference) rates of discount that were quoted above. The highest of these, for the whole of this century, is 2.1 per cent per annum. The Review does not dwell on the fact that, everywhere in the world, such relatively low real rates of return are not now characteristic of other investments. While it is true that the minimum acceptable rates of return for investment projects across the world are not known with any precision, and may well differ considerably, there is no doubt that they are typically much higher in the private sector; and even for public sector projects, most public enterprises and governments would probably look for higher real returns on expenditure than 2.1 per cent. The British Treasury, as noted above, recommends using a rate of 3.5 per cent with a full sensitivity analysis. This figure appears as low in relation to the practice of other OECD member countries for which evidence is available, as also of international lending agencies.[130]

When the marginal rate of return on investments exceeds some officially specified social time preference rate of discount, as in this case, there is a strong argument for using in public expenditure projects the higher of the two rates, since the use of dual criteria opens up the possibility that investments with relatively low returns will crowd out others that would be more beneficial. The risk is all the greater if, as is the case with the Stern Review's recommended course of action, the specially favoured measures, projects and programmes are worldwide and large scale.

This problem of dual criteria has been recognised by William Cline, in a study which is in many ways a precursor of the Review. Like the Review, he advocates a low social time preference rate of discount for evaluating climate-change-related expenditures; but unlike the Review, he faces up to the issue of crowding out. His solution is to apply a 'shadow price of capital', so that insofar as mitigation expenditures are thought to displace higher-yielding investments, their initial costs are adjusted upwards: he suggests a mark-up of 60 per cent.[131] Any such procedure, if accepted as valid, would of course serve to push up significantly the true estimated costs of mitigation. Although such a result is arguably implied by its own advocacy of dual expenditure criteria, it is not mentioned in the Review.

4. The choice of policy instruments

The Review raises a great many issues of policy, one of which we have just referred to. Here we focus mainly on the choice of policy instruments, an aspect which the Review considers at length. We end the section with a brief comment on what one might term the policy orientation of the Review.

Prices versus quantities

Moving the discussion to means, rather than ends, brings up another example in which the Review positions itself as an implausible outlier against the specialist literature. Section 14.4 ('Efficiency under uncertainty') presents a standard treatment of the question of instrument choice in the presence of uncertainty over damages and abatement costs. The Report correctly points out that, for the case of carbon dioxide, the marginal damages curve is relatively flat and the marginal abatement cost curve is relatively steep, and the Weitzman-type analysis indicates that emissions pricing yields a smaller expected welfare loss than tradable quotas.

Combined with the literature on the low monetary value of damages, the available expert literature therefore implies that optimal carbon policy would be, at most, a small charge on each unit of CO_2 emissions. This in turn would imply a small initial but progressively increasing reduction in emissions below the business-as-usual case. When the secondorder costs and benefits ('active revenue recycling') associated with factor market distortions induced by the new carbon tax are also taken into account, even small departures from business-as-usual carbon emissions appear as welfare-reducing (Parry, Williams and Goulder 1999; Bovenberg and Goulder 1996).

These arguments would lead to the conclusion that picking a carbon price is economically more sensible than picking a quantity, and that such a price would initially be likely to be relatively low. Such a conclusion, however – and bearing in mind the difficulty in achieving international agreement on carbon taxation – is not compatible with the 'need to take strong action now' asserted in the first sentence of the Review, and the implication that regulators should set a hard cap on emissions well below current levels.

Perhaps aware that the logic leads away from emission caps, the Review mounts a novel argument, based on a single, recently published conjecture that, in the future, what is currently believed about the relative slopes of the marginal damage and marginal abatement cost curves will be reversed.

Figure B in Box 14.1 asserts that while marginal costs of emission reductions will become very low, marginal damages due to carbon dioxide emissions will suddenly become very steep. The Review defends the idea that marginal costs will radically decline by invoking a vague notion that technology will change. The argument that the marginal damages curve will become steep is not defended: instead, on p. 314 the reader is referred to Chapter 13 for the discussion. In that chapter (p. 293) there is a list of conjectured horrors – hundreds of millions dead, social upheaval, etc. – leading on to the assertion that

> The expected impacts of climate change on well-being in the broadest sense are likely to accelerate as the stock of greenhouse gases increases, as argued in Chapter 3. The expected benefits of extra mitigation will therefore increase with the stabilisation level.7

Yet the footnote here contains text which goes against the point being made:

> One characteristic of the climate physics works in the opposite direction: the expected rise in temperature is a function of the *proportional* increase in the stock of greenhouse gases, not its *absolute* increase.

In other words, additional units of CO_2 in the atmosphere have an effect that goes with the logarithm of the level of CO_2, so that constant increments of CO_2 have diminishing marginal effect. This in turn implies that annual emissions have diminishing marginal impact, even in the long run.

We conclude, therefore, that the premise of the policy conclusions in Chapter 14 is false even on the Review's own reading of the evidence. The Review conjectures that the relative slopes of the marginal damages and marginal abatement cost curves will reverse, even while acknowledging that this is at odds with the available evidence. We would add that if the Review is correct, that foreseeable technologies will radically reduce the cost of carbon emission abatement in the near future, this is an argument for *delaying* abatement, not hurrying into it.

The Review appears to favour carbon trading, in part because it could involve transfers to developing counties. But very little account has been taken of the practical problems of implementing satisfactory systems, in particular setting up auctions or dealing properly with the initial allocation of emissions caps. These problems would be particularly acute at international level.

In principle, there is a place for 'market instruments' such as carbon taxes or carbon trading. Carbon taxes, for example, are transparent. It is relatively easy to ensure that they are levied widely – on individuals as well as companies. They have the merit that levels can be changed in response to improved knowledge. Their initial level would inevitably be arbitrary, but they could be introduced at a relatively low rate and raised as knowledge of carbon damage and the effectiveness of taxes accrues. Provided that proper explanations are given for changes, appropriate expectations can be created. And as noted in Section 2 above, carbon taxes would provide revenue for the public finances and make it possible to reduce other taxes or, say, to provide resources for other 'green' policies.

There could well be political resistance to carbon taxes – such as the blockages and motorway 'go-slows' in France and the UK in 2000; but acceptance or not of such taxes is a proper test of the willingness of people to support the policies that would lead to lower emissions.

Carbon trading likewise requires initial arbitrary decisions – in its case, on the 'desirable' levels of emissions to be achieved and their allocation to emitters. It is one thing to apply limits to a relatively small level of emitters, say large carbon using companies, and is another to apply them to all emitters, including the personal sector. Yet if limits are applied arbitrarily or unevenly, much of the benefit of using an economic instrument is lost.

Both rules and administrative mechanisms need to be devised for the working of any market for trading permits; and if there is to be international trading, all the governments concerned need to act objectively and fairly, and to be seen to be acting objectively and fairly.

Trading today is very far from being universal: it is being applied only to a limited number of emitters. For example, the EU Emissions Trading Scheme, in its phase one, covers less than 40% of relevant emissions. In the present state of knowledge, there is no way of setting the right levels, at either the national or the European level – and if they are subsequently changed, this creates uncertainty about arrangements that work only because of their longer-term incentives.

Furthermore, until governments start to auction or otherwise charge for the initial level, allocations will typically involve presenting substantial benefits to existing emitters or their suppliers. The Review advocates the use of auctions to allocate the 'desirable' amount of emissions, but the design of an auction for a large number of emitters would be complex and contentious. Until auctions are in place, carbon trading scores badly on transparency. The overall economic costs may be high, albeit disguised. Or the allocations may be so generous that costs are low, but so are the overall reductions in emissions after taking account of the gains that individuals may make by trading what is allocated to them.

There is some empirical evidence on the performance of trading schemes. In relation to the UK Emissions Trading Scheme, the world's first large-scale greenhouse gas trading scheme, that began in 2002, Smith & Swierzbinski (2006) argue that the initial setting of targets for emissions can be the Achilles' heel of emissions trading. The authorities are at an informational disadvantage and the price of making trading arrangements acceptable is to start in generous mode, giving substantial benefits to existing high emitters. They further conclude that adjustment of initial error is both difficult and potentially costly. Efficient functioning of the market requires stability and confidence about current and future property rights, and the repurchasing of rights once allocated can be costly.

The optimal policy target

In Section 13.7 of the Review, the issue is raised of identifying an optimal concentration of 'greenhouse gases'. The Review cites a group of studies (by Nordhaus and Boyer; Tol; and Manne and Richels) and concedes (p. 298) that they all lead to the same conclusion:

> These studies recommend that greenhouse gas emissions be reduced below business-as-usual forecasts, but the reductions suggested have been modest.

But once again, the expert literature is promptly set aside on the basis of the Review's own contrary opinion (p. 298):

> However, the optimal amount of mitigation may in fact be greater than these studies have suggested.

In this context, as elsewhere, conjectural grounds are given as to why the experts who have studied the issue hitherto have all missed the salient features to which only the Review is privy, and which yield an entirely different conclusion, namely that deep emissions cuts are optimal. But the peer-reviewed literature, even that portion surveyed in the Review, suggests that an emissions charge equal to marginal damages – at most, say of US$10 per ton of carbon – is the most aggressive aggregate emissions control policy that could be justified. Because of the steepness of the marginal abatement cost curve, this implies that most countries implementing such a policy would initially reduce emissions only slightly – although the cumulative effect over the longer term would be much greater. Of course, if the path of abatement costs is not as steep as is currently thought, a small CO_2 tax might actually induce large emission reductions. However, to propose deep emissions cuts on that conjecture alone would be to make the mistake associated with the prices-versus-quantities analysis described above. In the case of carbon emissions, the social costs associated with policy uncertainty are minimized by choosing an emissions price and letting the market determine the quantity.

The role of government

While the Review makes many allusions to imperfections and failures in markets, it makes no mention even of the possibility of government failure: in this connection, no reference is made to the arguments and findings of public choice theory. The consequence of ignoring the limits and failings of political action is serious, because the Review points to the need for such action to be undertaken on a grand scale, both nationally and internationally.

While prescribing a greatly expanded role for governments, the Review has failed to think through what could be the considerable problems of defining that role and carrying it into effect. A leading instance is to be found in its recommendation, noted above, that a special and much lower rate of discount should be used for mitigation projects alone. A possible consequence of using such low discount rates, relative to those used in the private sector, is that governments would find themselves faced with an array of potential investments that arguably 'should' be undertaken but which the private sector would not find worthwhile. In such situations, ensuring that the investments were made would require heavy state involvement. Governments would be compelled either to assign to public authorities the responsibility of carrying out the projects in question or to assume the task of designing and putting in place the necessary incentives for private businesses to undertake them; and both these courses of action would involve an expansion of the public sector. The problems that could arise from the adoption of a dual discount rate are not faced in the Review.

5. Missing elements

Despite its considerable bulk, the Stern Review is far from being a complete and well-rounded survey of its subject. The main reason for this is the pervasive bias which we and our scientific colleagues have both noted, and which has led to the disregard or undervaluing of sources which suggest a different view of those aspects of its subject-matter that the Review considers. But a further limitation of the Review is that there are aspects which it fails to cover, or even to recognise as pertinent. One such aspect, just noted, is that it does not face up to the problems that may arise from 'government failure'. But this is by no means the only instance where relevant topics and concerns are passed over.

A serious omission concerns an issue which goes beyond economics, and has been raised and discussed in Part I above. Our scientific colleagues have noted there the failures of due disclosure, still unacknowledged and unremedied, that have characterised published and peer-reviewed work which the IPCC and its member governments have drawn on. Neither the failures themselves nor the publications which have exposed them are mentioned in the Review: it simply turns a blind eye to evidence that might put in question any elements of 'the science'.[132] The procedural flaws which it thus disregards put in question the IPCC process as a whole, and further undermine any claim that 'the scientific evidence is now overwhelming'.

A further respect in which the IPCC process is open to question is the treatment within it of economic issues. In this connection, two of us (Castles and Henderson) have pointed to flaws both in the SRES and more broadly. These arguments receive only passing and misleading mention in the Review. Contrary to what is said or implied in the text (pp. 182 and 188), this critique of the SRES is by no means confined to the emissions projections made in the report, while what it says about the IPCC – as also the United Nations Environment Programme, which is one of the IPCC's two parent agencies – extends well beyond the scenarios. Further – and here again there is a link with Part I – these authors have made the point, in the context of the IPCC process, that peer review offers no safeguard against dubious assumptions, arguments and conclusions if the peers are largely drawn from the same restricted professional milieu. This aspect also is not touched on in the Review. An article in which the whole of this particular debate was reviewed and taken further (Henderson 2005) is not mentioned in the Review or included in its list of references.[133]

Both these topics – the question of disclosure, and the treatment of economic issues within the IPCC process – were considered in the wide-ranging report, likewise entitled 'The economics of climate change', which was prepared by the House of Lords Select Committee on Economic Affairs and published in July 2005.[134] The report was accompanied by a separate and substantial volume containing the written and oral evidence submitted to the Committee. Despite its having treated the identical subject at length, and in a way that evoked widespread attention, the Select Committee report does not find a place among the 1,100 or so references that are listed in the Review. This is an extraordinary omission.

A notable feature of the Select Committee report was the concerns that it expressed about the IPCC. Given the general credibility which the Panel has acquired, it is remarkable that a group of eminent, experienced and responsible persons, drawn from a national legislative body and spanning the political spectrum, with the help of an internationally recognised expert adviser, and after taking and weighing evidence, should have published a considered and unanimous report in which such concerns are prominently voiced.

The Stern Review makes no reference to the issues thus raised. It takes the established official process of inquiry and assessment, including the contribution of the IPCC, as given and fully trustworthy. The possibility that the process could be improved is not entertained. This missing dimension severely limits the usefulness of the Review as a guide to policy. Its uncritical acceptance of officially sponsored sources helps to explain its strong and pervasive bias, since much the same areas and instances of bias, though often in less extreme and unqualified form, are to be seen on the part of its mentors.

We believe – and our scientific colleagues concur – that the House of Lords Select Committee was right to raise these questions, and the Stern Review is wrong to ignore them. There is a serious problem here. Although it provides for substantial, well organised and worldwide expert participation, the IPCC process is far from being a model of rigour, inclusiveness and impartiality: it is in fact deeply flawed. Its member governments either fail to notice the flaws or view them with a tolerant eye. There is an urgent need today to build up a sounder basis than now exists for reviewing and assessing issues relating to climate change.[135]

6. Conclusions

Our main conclusions coincide with, and serve to confirm and reinforce, those reached by our scientific colleagues in Part I above. Like them, we would emphasise in particular two interrelated features of the Stern Review:

- it greatly understates the extent of uncertainty as to possible developments, in highly complex systems that are not well understood, over a period of two centuries or more

- its treatment of sources and evidence is persistently selective and biased.

These twin features have combined to make the Review a vehicle for speculative alarmism.

We also endorse, from our own analysis, the judgement of our colleagues that the Review:

- mishandles data

- gives too little attention to actual observation and evidence, as distinct-from the results of model-based exercises

- takes no account of the failures of due disclosure, and the chronic limitations of peer reviewing, that have been characteristic of work relating to climate change which governments have commissioned and drawn on.

As to specifically economic aspects, we have noted among other weaknesses that the Review:

- systematically overstates projected costs of climate change, partlythough by no means wholly as a result of its failure to acknowledge the scope for long-term adaptation to possible global warming

- underestimates the likely cost – including to the world's poor – of the-drastic global mitigation programme that it calls for

- proposes worldwide adoption of a specially low rate of interest for discounting the costs and benefits of mitigation, on the basis of inadequate analysis and without regard for the problems and risks that would result.

So far from being an authoritative guide to the economics of climate change, the Review is deeply flawed. It does not provide a basis for informed and responsible policies.

Annex: The Stern Review and the IPCC Scenarios

In this Annex, we examine the Stern Review's uncritical use of the IPCC's scenarios of future emissions of greenhouse gases, as published in the Panel's *Special Report on Emissions Scenarios* (SRES).

The detailed analysis in the Review's assessments of the potential impacts of climate change relies upon 'a series of papers prepared by Prof. Martin Parry and colleagues ('FastTrack')' which, according to the Review, represents 'one of the few that clearly sets out the assumptions used and explores different sources of uncertainty' (p. 61).

In choosing to use only four of the SRES scenarios in their analysis, Professor Parry and his colleagues disregarded one of the most important sources of uncertainty in the assessment of climate change impacts: the differing possibilities for the developments of energy technologies. The need to take these alternatives into account had been stressed in the Summary for Policymakers of the SRES:

> The *six* scenario groups – the three scenario families A2, B1, and B2, plus three groups within the A1 scenario family, A1B, A1FI, and A1T – and four cumulative emissions categories were developed as *the smallest subsets of SRES scenarios that capture the range of uncertainties* associated with driving forces and emissions. (SRES, p. 11, emphases added.)

Both the 'FastTrack' exercise and the Stern Review ignore two of the three groups within the A1 scenario family, and present the A1FI scenario as *the* emissions scenario in that family: see, for example, the tabulation of the demographic and economic data relating to the A1 scenario in Box 3.2 (p. 61) of the Review, and the presentation of more than 200 additional millions as at risk of hunger under a hypothetical temperature increase for 'A1' of over 4°C in Figure 3.6 (b) on p. 73. If the A1T scenario had been used instead of the A1FI scenario, the temperature increase on the horizontal scale and the 'additional millions at risk' on the vertical scale would both have been much smaller.

Importantly, the Terms of Reference of the SRES required that '*none* of the scenarios in the set includes any future policies that explicitly address additional climate change initiatives', so that 'For example, no scenarios are included that explicitly assume implementation of the emissions targets in the UNFCCC and the Kyoto Protocol' (SRES, p. 23, emphasis in original).

By choosing to analyse the impacts of the 'very high' economic growth scenario using only the A1FI (fossil fuel intensive) scenario, and disregarding other scenarios that share similar economic growth assumptions but have much lower levels of emissions, the 'FastTrack' studies and the Stern Review present a fundamentally distorted view of the prospective impacts of climate change in the absence of mitigation policies.

This can be seen most readily by noting that the omitted A1T emissions scenario assumes a higher rate of economic growth, and a higher level of global GDP in 2100, than any of the four scenarios used in the 'FastTrack' studies; but that the cumulative level of emissions under this scenario, and the projected increase in global-mean temperatures that goes with it, are *lower* than under the B2 scenario – even though the latter scenario assumes the lowest rate of economic growth, and the lowest global GDP in 2100, of the four scenarios that are used in the 'FastTrack' analyses.[136] By relying entirely upon the A1FI variant of the A1 scenario family and ignoring the A1T variant of the same family, the Stern Review presents it as inevitable that, if rapid economic growth continues, emissions will continue to escalate in the absence of climate policies.

This view does not sit easily with the following statement in the SRES Summary for Policymakers:

> [T]here are scenarios with high per capita incomes in all regions that lead to high CO_2 emissions (e.g., in the high-growth, fossil fuel intensive scenario group A1FI)...[And] there are scenarios with high per capita incomes that lead to low emissions (e.g., the A1T scenario group or the B1 scenario family). (p. 11)

Further, the Review's interpretation is certainly inconsistent with the argument by 15 members of the SRES writing team in their initial response to the Castles and Henderson critique:

> The fact that 17 out of the 40 SRES scenarios explore alternative technological development pathways under a high growth... scenario family A1 does not constitute a statement that such scenarios should be considered more likely than others with a less dynamic technological and economic development outlook, nor that a similar large number of technological 'bifurcation' scenarios would not be possible in any of the other three scenario families... The special value of the criticized A1 and B1 scenarios resides precisely in the insight that such an income gap closure [between

average incomes in developing and developed countries] might not necessarily be associated with extremely high GHG emissions *but could also evolve even in the absence of climate policies with comparatively low emissions* (as for instance in the technologically optimistic A1T and B1T scenarios). (Nakicenovic *et al.*, 2003, 'IPCC SRES Revisited: A Response', *Energy & Environment*, 14 (2 & 3): 195–96, emphasis added.)

It follows that the Review's claim that 'All but one SRES *storyline* envisage a concentration level [of greenhouse gases] well in excess of 650 ppm CO_2e by [the end of the century]' (p. 177, emphasis added) reveals a fundamental misreading of the SRES. The storylines presented in the Report do not in themselves envisage specific concentration levels at particular times in the future: these levels are also a function of the assumed technological development pathway.[137]

By focusing on the fossil fuel intensive variant of the A1 scenario, and ignoring the technologically optimistic variants or possible variants of the other scenario families, the Review fails to consider the possibility that continuing growth in global emissions is not inevitable, even in the absence of climate policies.

The Review asserts that 'the likelihood of economic growth slowing sufficiently to reverse emissions growth by itself is small' (p. 182). This again reveals a misunderstanding of the SRES scenarios, all of which are presented as 'equally valid with no assigned probabilities of occurrence' (SRES, Box SPM-1, p. 4). Many of the scenarios project a reversal in emissions growth in the course of the century.

Besides presenting a distorted view, the Review is slipshod in its reporting of the SRES results. For example, the statement that the growth in world GDP under the SRES scenarios is projected 'to continue at between 2 and 3% per year' (p. 182 of the Review) cannot be reconciled with the growth rate of '3.5% p.a.' reported for the A1FI scenario in the table in Box 3.2 (p. 61). The difference is not trivial: over the 110-year time span of the SRES projections, growth at an average rate of 3.5% annually yields a GDP level in 2100 which is 70% greater than the level resulting from an average growth rate of 3.0% annually over the same period. The difference between the projected GDP in 2100 under a 3.5% growth rate from 1990 onwards and that resulting from a 3.0% growth rate over the same period is equivalent to nearly 20 times the level of global GDP in the base year of 1990.

The table in the Review's Box 3.2 reports a projected level of world GDP in 2100 under the A1FI scenario of $550 trillion in 1990 US $. The correct figure, as shown by the SRES (p. 436), is $525 trillion.

Finally, all of the estimates and projections of regional and global GDP in the SRES are distorted as a result of the use of exchange-rate-based conversions as if they measured differences in output across countries. The use of these flawed estimates and projections in the 'FastTracks' project raises in itself serious questions about the validity of the assessments of climate change impacts both in that exercise and in the Stern Review.

References

Anderson, Dennis (2006), 'Costs and finance of carbon abatement in the energy sector', paper for the Stern Review, available at www.sternreview.org.uk

Barker, T., M. S. Qureshi, and J. Kohler (2006), 'The costs of greenhouse gas mitigation with induced technological change: A meta-analysis of estimates in the literature', 4CMR, Cambridge Centre for Climate Change Mitigation Research.

Bovenberg, A. Lans, and Lawrence H. Goulder (1996), 'Optimal environmental taxation in the presence of other taxes: General-equilibrium analyses', *American Economic Review*, 86 (4): 985–1000.

Bovenberg, A. Lans, and Ruud A. de Mooij (1994), 'Environmental levies and distortionary taxation', *American Economic Review*, 84: 1085–9.

British Petroleum (2006), *Statistical Review of World Energy*, June, and www.bp.com/statisticalreview

Castles, Ian, and David Henderson (2003), 'The IPCC emissions scenarios: An economic–statistical critique', *Energy & Environment*, 14 (2 & 3): 173.

Cline, William R. (1992), *The Economics of Global Warming*, Washington, DC, Institute of International Economics.

Cline, William R. (2004), 'Climate change', chapter 1 of Bjørn Lomborg (ed.), *Global Crises, Global Solutions*, Cambridge University Press.

Dasgupta, P. (2006), 'Comments on the Stern Review's Economics of Climate Change', Presentation at the Foundation for Science and Technology at the Royal Society, London.

Fullerton, Don (1997), 'Environmental levies and distortionary taxation: Comment', *American Economic Review*, 87 (1): 245–251.

Helm, Dieter (2003), *Energy, The State and The Market*, Oxford University Press.

Henderson, David (2005), 'SRES, IPCC, and the treatment of economic issues: What has emerged?', *Energy and Environment*, 16 (3 & 4).

Henderson, David (2006), 'Governments and climate change issues: The case for a new approach', *Energy and Environment*, 17 (4).

House of Lords Select Committee on Economic Affairs (2005), *The Economics of Climate Change*, Volume I: Report; Volume II: Evidence, London, The Stationery Office.

McIntyre, Stephen, and Ross McKitrick (2003), 'Corrections to the Mann et al. (1998) Proxy Data Base and Northern Hemisphere Average Temperature Series', *Energy and Environment*, 14 (6): 751–771.

McIntyre, Stephen, and Ross McKitrick (2005), 'The M&M critique of the MBH98 Northern Hemisphere Climate Index: Update and Implications', *Energy and Environment,* 16 (1): 69–100.

McIntyre, Stephen, and Ross McKitrick (2005), 'Hockey sticks, principal components and spurious significance', *Geophysical Research Letters,* 32 (3), L03710 10.1029/2004GL021750, 12 February 2005.

McKitrick, Ross R. (2006), 'Bringing balance, disclosure and due diligence into science-based policymaking', in Porter, Jene (ed.), *Public Science in Liberal Democracy: The Challenge to Science and Democracy*, University of Toronto Press.

Manne, A., and R. Richels (1995), 'The greenhouse debate: Economic efficiency, burden-sharing and hedging strategies', *The Energy Journal,* 16 (4).

Nordhaus, William (2006), 'The *Stern Review* on the Economics of Climate Change', http://nordhaus.econ.yale.edu/SternReviewD2.pdf

Nordhaus, William, and J. G. Boyer (2000), *Warming the World: The Economics of the Greenhouse Effect*, MIT Press.

Parry, Ian W. H. (1995), 'Pollution taxes and revenue recycling', *Journal of Environmental Economics and Management,* 29: S64–77.

Parry, Ian, Roberton C. Williams III, and Lawrence H. Goulder (1999), 'When can carbon abatement policies increase welfare? The fundamental role of distorted factor markets', *Journal of Environmental Economics and Management,* 37: 52–84.

Robinson, Colin (1988), 'Britain's energy market', *The Economic Review,* 5 (3), January.

Sandmo, Agnar (1975), 'Optimal taxation in the presence of externalities', *Swedish Journal of Economics,* 77 (1): 86–98.

Smith, Stephen, and Joseph Swierzbinski (2006), 'Assessing the performance of the UK emissions trading scheme', revised submission to *Environmental and Resource Economics*, October.

Spackman, Michael (2001), 'Public investment and discounting in European Union member states', published in *OECD Journal on Budgeting,* 1 (2).

Tol, Richard S. J. (1997), 'On the optimal control of carbon dioxide emissions: An application of FUND', *Environmental Modelling and Assessment,* 2.

Tol, Richard S. J. (2005), 'The marginal damage costs of carbon dioxide emissions: An assessment of the uncertainties', *Energy Policy,* 33.

Tol, Richard S. J., and Gary Yohe (2006), 'A Review of the *Stern Review*', *World Economics,* 7 (4), October–December.

Warren, R., et al. (2006), 'Spotlighting impacts functions in integrated assessment models', Norwich, Tyndall Centre for Climate Change Research Working Paper 91.

Watkiss, P., et al. (2005), 'Methodological approaches for using social cost of carbon estimates in policy assessment', Final Report, AEA Technology Environment, Culham.

The Authors

Part I: The science

Bob Carter is a palaeontologist, stratigrapher, marine geologist and environmental scientist with degrees from the University of Otago (NZ; BSc Hons) and Cambridge University (UK; PhD). He has held staff positions at the University of Otago (Dunedin) and James Cook University (Townsville), where he was Head of the School of Earth Sciences 1981–1999 and an Adjunct Research Professor thereafter. He has published research papers on climate change, sea-level change, palaeontology and stratigraphy, based on field studies of Cenozoic sediments from the Australasian region and supported by grants from the Australian Research Council (ARC). In 1998, he was Co-Chief Scientist on Ocean Drilling Leg 181, Southwest Pacific Gateways, a cruise that made fundamental contributions to our knowledge of climate change in southern midlatitudes. He receives no research funding from special interest organisations such as environmental groups, energy companies or government departments.

Chris de Freitas is a climate scientist in the School of Geography, Geology and Environmental Science at the University of Auckland, where he has been Head of Science and Technology at the Tamaki campus and Pro Vice Chancellor. He has Bachelors and Masters degrees from the University of Toronto and a PhD from the University of Queensland as a Commonwealth Scholar. For 10 years he was as an editor of the international journal *Climate Research*. He is an advocate of open and well-informed reporting on scientific issues. In recognition of this, he has three times been the recipient of the New Zealand Association of Scientists Science Communicator Award.

Indur M. Goklany is a science and technology policy analyst at the US Department of the Interior. In 30-plus years in government, think tanks, and the private sector, he has written three books and over a hundred monographs, book chapters and papers on topics ranging from climate change, human wellbeing, and technological change to biotechnology, sustainable development and adaptation. He represented the US at the Intergovernmental Panel on Climate Change, and at the negotiations leading to the UN Framework Convention on Climate Change. He was the principal author of the Resource Use and Management Subgroup report in the IPCC's First Assessment. In the 1980s, he managed EPA's fledgling emission trading program before that became popular. His degrees are in Electrical Engineering (B.Tech, Indian Institute of Technology, Bombay; M.S., Ph.D., Michigan State University). Views expressed here do not necessarily reflect those of the US government or any of its units.

David Holland is an engineer, and a member of the Institution of Engineering and Technology. He has followed the scientific debate over the human contribution to global warming for many years and submitted written evidence to the 2005 House of Lords Enquiry into the Economics of Climate Change.

Richard S. Lindzen has been the Alfred P. Sloan Professor of Atmospheric Sciences at the Massachusetts Institute of Technology since 1983. Prior to his present position, he held professorships at Harvard and the University of Chicago. His A.B., S.M. and Ph.D. are from Harvard. He is a member of the National Academy of Sciences, the Norwegian Academy of Sciences and Letters, and the American Academy of Arts and Sciences. He is also a fellow of the American Meteorological Society and the American Geophysical Union. He is the recipient of various awards, and has served on numerous committees and panels, including service as a lead author for the IPCC Third Assessment Report. He is the author or coauthor of three books and over 200 papers. His current research is on climate sensitivity, atmospheric convection and on the general circulation of the atmosphere.

Part II: Economic aspects

Sir Ian Byatt is Chairman of the Water Industry Commission for Scotland, a Senior Associate with Frontier Economics and an Honorary Professor at Birmingham University. He was previously Director General of Water Services (OFWAT) and, before that, Deputy Economic Adviser to HM Treasury.

Ian Castles is a former Head of the Australian Bureau of Statistics, and is currently a Visiting Fellow in the Asia Pacific School of Economics and Government at the Australian National University, Canberra.

Indur M. Goklany (see above).

David Henderson is a former Head of the Economics and Statistics Department of the OECD, and is currently a Visiting Professor at the Westminster Business School, London.

Lord Lawson of Blaby[†] is a former British Chancellor of the Exchequer, and is currently a member of the House of Lords Select Committee on Economic Affairs.

[†] Lord Lawson and Lord Skidelsky were signatories of the 2005 report from the Select Committee on Economic Affairs of the House of Lords on 'The Economics of Climate Change'. All the rest of the Part II authors submitted evidence to the Select Committee, to the Stern Review in its opening stages, or to both.

Ross McKitrick is Associate Professor of Economics at Guelph University, Ontario, Canada, and has written extensively on issues relating to climate change. He was one of twelve experts from around the world asked to present evidence to the US National Academy of Sciences Expert Panel on Millennial Paleoclimate Reconstructions. He is the joint author (with Chris Essex) of *Taken By Storm: The Troubled Science, Policy and Politics of Global Warming* (Key Porter Books), the second edition of which will soon be published.

Julian Morris is Executive Director of the International Policy Network in London and a Visiting Professor at the University of Buckingham.

Sir Alan Peacock is Honorary Professor of Public Finance at Heriot Watt University and a former Chief Economic Adviser to the Department of Trade and Industry.

Colin Robinson is Emeritus Professor of Economics, University of Surrey, and is a recipient of the International Association for Energy Economics award for 'Outstanding Contributions to the Profession of Energy Economics and its Literature'.

Lord Skidelsky[†] is Professor of Political Economy at the University of Warwick, and author of the awardwinning biography of John Maynard Keynes. He is currently a member of the House of Lords Select Committee on Economic Affairs.

Economists and Climate Science: A Critique

Originally published in World Economics, March 2009, and reproduced with permission.

Theme and targets

In this paper I question the characteristic treatment of climate change issues by fellow economists, as seen in recent articles, books and reports. The focus of the paper, however, is not on economics. My main theme is what I see as the uncritical and over-presumptive way in which these various sources have dealt with the scientific aspects of the subject. Although I also refer to other illustrative cases, the chief specific targets of criticism are six recent and influential publications. Three of these are by leading and widely respected individual authors. They are:

- William Nordhaus's book *A Question of Balance* (2008)

- Martin Weitzman's article entitled 'On modeling and interpreting the economics of catastrophic climate change' (2009)

- Dieter Helm's article entitled 'Climate-change policy: why has so little been achieved?' (2008)

Alongside this trio I place two prominent large-scale officially sponsored though independent reviews:

- the 700-page Stern review, *The Economics of Climate Change*, by Nicholas (now Lord) Stern and others, commissioned by the British government and published in 2007

- the 600-page *Garnaut Climate Change Review*, authored by Ross Garnaut, commissioned by the state and territorial governments of Australia with the later participation of the commonwealth government, and published in 2008.

Last on the list is the special chapter on climate change issues that formed part of the April 2008 issue of the International Monetary Fund's (IMF) twice-yearly flagship publication, *World Economic Outlook.**

It is an unusual procedure for an economist to criticise what fellow economists have said, or failed to say, about a subject area that is neither his nor theirs. I therefore begin by setting the issues that I raise in the wider context of the current climate change debate.

Background and context

A spectrum of opinions

In relation to climate change issues, there exists a widely shared diagnosis and prescription, a body of *received opinion* shared by the great majority of governments and by many of their citizens. The core of received opinion, briefly summarised, is that warming caused by human activities, through rising emissions of (so-called) 'greenhouse gases', has already become the main influence on global surface temperatures; that global warming can be expected to proceed further, unless effective measures are put in place to prevent this; that such a general unconstrained rise in global temperatures would increasingly carry with it serious risks, with the possibility of developments that could be classed as catastrophic; and that in consequence further prompt, sustained and worldwide governmental action is called for to limit the extent of warming and deal with its possible consequences. The action would chiefly take the form of 'mitigation' – that is, of measures to curb emissions of greenhouse gases in general and CO_2 in particular. Predictably, received opinion is not universally shared. Both diagnosis and prescription remain subject to challenge by a varied collection of doubters, sceptics, questioners, critics, nonconformists, non-subscribers – in a word, *dissenters*. Against them, and greatly outnumbering them, are arrayed what I term the *upholders* of received opinion. Within both groups, again predictably, there are different schools of thought: a whole spectrum of opinions can be identified. At one end, there are what may be termed *strong* or *full - blown* upholders, the dark greens so to speak. Prominent among these are Lord

---

*I have commented on the Stern review in Byatt *et al.* (2006), as a joint author, and in Henderson (2007a); on the IMF's involvement in Henderson (2007b, 2008a); and on the Draft Report of the Garnaut Review in Henderson (2008b). At various points below I have drawn on these pieces without specific attribution.

Stern and his co-authors: the Stern Review takes the position (2007, p. xv) that prospective warming 'is a serious global threat' and 'demands an urgent global response'. At the other end of the spectrum, strong dissenters – the dark blues – argue that such warming, if indeed its extent can be shown to be significant, is not a cause for alarm or concern: hence mitigation measures should be eschewed – or discontinued, where they are now in place. In between these two far removed positions, there are upholders and dissenters who hold more *limited* or *qualified* beliefs; and in the middle there is sometimes common ground, so that the basic dividing line can become blurred.[†] Each of the various subject areas involved, including economics, has its own distinctive spectrum. More of this below.

A consensus and its basis

Received opinion is reflected in an *official policy consensus*. With few exceptions, governments across the world are committed to the view that anthropogenic global warming (from now on, AGW) constitutes a serious problem that requires official action at both national and international level.

This official consensus is not new. Climate change issues have been on the international agenda for 20 years or more, and it is now practically 17 years since governments decided, collectively and almost unanimously, that determined steps should be taken to deal with what they agreed was a major problem. The decisive collective commitment was made in 1992, through the United Nations Framework convention on climate change. The convention specifies, using language that goes back to a 1990 Ministerial Declaration, that its 'ultimate objective' is:

> To achieve... stabilization of greenhouse gas emissions in the atmosphere at a level that would prevent dangerous anthropogenic interference with the climate system.

That agreed objective remains in place today.

Since 1992, many governments have acted, through what is now a wide range of measures and programmes, to curb emissions of CO_2. On the international scene, through the Kyoto Protocol, 'Annex I' countries have undertaken to meet specific targets for emissions reductions, and at the coming major in-

---

[†] One could alternatively use the terms 'radical' and 'moderate' to distinguish the extremes from the intermediate positions, but the latter term has too favourable a connotation, so that more neutral language seems better. of course, the above fourfold classification is no more than a first rough approximation. There are many schools of thought and shades of opinion.

ternational gathering in copenhagen (December 2009) the governments of the world will be considering what further measures, possibly involving developing countries also, might extend or replace the Protocol after its present commitment period expires in 2012.

In taking this course, governments have met with widespread public approval. Within the political domain, there has been virtually unanimous cross-party agreement. Beyond it, strong support has come from media commentators, representative scientific bodies including the royal Society, environmental advocacy groups (the non-governmental organisations), and, increasingly, large business enterprises. Further, and as noted below, there is considerable support for the official consensus position among economists.

What was it that persuaded governments across the world, almost two decades ago, to take the possible dangers of AGW so seriously, and what is it that has caused them to maintain and even intensify their concerns, with a good deal of public support? I think the answer is straightforward. From the start the main influence was, as it still is, the scientific advice provided through what I call the *official advisory process*.

That advice can and does come from many sources; but the main single channel for it, indeed the only channel of advice for governments *collectively*, has been the series of massive and wide-ranging Assessment Reports produced by the Intergovernmental Panel on Climate Change (IPCC). The most recent of these, referred to for short as AR4, was completed and published in the course of 2007. It chiefly comprises the lengthy separate volumes brought out by each of the Panel's three Working Groups: WGI deals with issues of climate science, WGII with the prospective impacts of possible global warming, and WGIII with mitigation measures. The various documents that make up AR4 come to around 3,000 pages, and some 2,500 experts – authors, contributors and reviewers – were directly involved in preparing them. I refer to these persons as the *expert network*. Although the two are often confused, the network is quite distinct from the Panel.

The three post-1992 Assessment Reports, including AR4, have served to confirm and reinforce the agreed position that governments arrived at when they adopted the Framework Convention.

The IPCC does not itself undertake or commission research. The Assessment Reports review and draw on already published work, so that the Panel's contribution forms only one element in the advisory process. All the same, the IPCC is influential and important in its own right. Its reports carry substantial weight, with public opinion as well as its member governments, because of their wide-ranging coverage of the issues and their extensive and ordered expert participation. In 2007 the Panel's work received further and conspicuous recognition through the award of the Nobel Peace Prize, which it shared with Al Gore.

Through its three working groups, the IPCC covers the whole range of topics relating to climate change, including economic aspects. However, what has chiefly carried weight throughout has been its presentation of climate science in the reports from WGI. For example, the citation for the Nobel award focuses on the way in which the Panel 'has created an ever-broader informed consensus about the connection between human activities and global warming'. Through the whole series of Assessment Reports, the reality of this connection has been taken, by governments and public opinion alike, as the IPCC's central message.

Support for this message, and praise for the IPCC's work, have come from scientists outside the field of climate science and also from leading scientific academies across the world. It is often claimed that there now exists a worldwide scientific consensus on climate change issues. For reasons that I will come to, such language leaves me uneasy. Nevertheless, I think it is correct to say that, alongside the official policy consensus (which *is* a reality), and providing much of its rationale and support, there exists a body of what can be termed *prevailing scientific opinion*.

To sum up: the core of received opinion, and its point of departure, is that scientific research, as reflected in the WGI reports, has provided increasingly firm and convincing evidence of the reality and the serious potential threat of AGW. That belief forms the basis for the official policy consensus and the widespread unofficial support for it.

A divided profession (1)

In relation to climate change issues, economists as usual are far from being of one mind. However, I believe that a clear majority of those who hold views on the subject broadly subscribe to received opinion. Evidence for this can be seen, for example, in both the Stern and Garnaut reviews; in the list of those economists (including four Nobel prize winners) whose endorsements of the Stern Review are printed there (2007, pp. ii–iii); in a public statement of December 2005 by 25 leading American academics; and in a similar statement of May 2007 signed by 271 university economists in Australia. All six authors and sources listed above, and criticised below, count as upholders, as also do various international agencies besides the IMF that have economic concerns and expertise, including the World Bank and the organisation for Economic co-operation and Development (OECD).

Some of the current differences within the profession relate to already familiar issues which arise in other areas of policy. A leading instance, and an important one in this context where distant possibilities are in question, is the choice of an appropriate rate of interest for discounting projected future costs and benefits. Thus for example, among our authors, both Nordhaus (2008) and Helm (2008) have questioned the low rate of interest that the Stern Review argued for; and by implication their criticisms apply also to the Garnaut Report, which here as elsewhere takes much the same line as Stern. On another key issue, Helm has argued (2008, p. 228) that 'the costs of mitigating climate change are likely to be significantly higher than in the Stern Report'. Again, Weitzman has posed a fundamental question of how far the characteristic economists' approach to questions of public policy, through the application of cost–benefit analysis, is appropriate to a situation in which there exists (2009, p. 2) 'a non-negligible probability of worldwide catastrophe', while Nordhaus (2008, pp. 146–147; 2009) has shown himself unconvinced by the argument and its implications.[‡]

While the differences just referred to are among upholders, there are also conflicting views within the dissenters' camp – in particular, between those who accept and those who reject the case for mitigation policies. On both sides of the dividing line, the resulting professional exchanges, though they often draw on arguments and evidence from other disciplines, generally take place within the recognised bounds of economic discourse. By contrast, the dividing line itself is of a different kind: it falls outside the accepted limits of our subject. The division between upholders and dissenters concerns the choice of a point of departure; and this choice depends on a judgement as to what conclusions it is appropriate to draw from arguments and evidence that are scientific rather than economic. received opinion among economists, as within most governments, takes as a basis for further analysis what it sees as firmly grounded scientific evidence and conclusions.

In the sections that now follow I give reasons for questioning this majority assessment. I have come to think that the present generally accepted treatment of scientific aspects by economists, as exemplified in the various sources that I quote below, is characterised by over-presumption, inadvertence and misplaced trust, and, in consequence by an unbalanced treatment of policy choices in which a key aspect is passed over.

[‡] The contention that cost–benefit analysis is not relevant to an evaluation of the extreme possibilities raised by AGW was put forward in 1992 by the philosopher John Broome, in a study entitled *Counting the Cost of Global Warming*.

Over-presumption

Misusing language

In all the six main sources treated here, as in many other places, the term 'climate change' is persistently misused. Here are some representative instances.

1. Nordhaus (2008, p. 4): 'alternative options for dealing with climate change'.

2. Weitzman (2009, p. 9): 'nightmare implications of climate change'.

3. Helm (2008, p. 220): 'the urgency of the climate change problem'.

4. Stern (2007, p. 65): 'climate change threatens the basic elements of life for people around the world.'

5. Garnaut (2008, p. xviii): 'climate change is a diabolical policy problem.'

6. IMF (2008, p. 133): 'climate change is a potentially catastrophic global externality.'

By way of reinforcing the point, here are some further specimens from other influential sources.

- Adair (Lord) Turner, Chair of the Committee on Climate Change, in a press statement of 1 December 2008: 'climate change poses a grave threat to human welfare, the environment and the economy.'[§]

- Amartya Sen, in the Stern Review (2007, p. ii): 'The stark prospects of climate change…'.

- The *Financial Times,* in a leading article of 27 January 2009: 'all countries need to fight climate change'.

- The OECD Secretariat, as the opening statement in a document of october 2008 specially prepared for ministers: 'climate change is confronting us with the fierce urgency of "now".'

In all these cases, as in countless others of their kind, what the authors are actually referring to is not climate change but AGW: they write as though the two could now be taken to be the same. This is grossly misleading. climate change can occur, has occurred, and may well be occurring now, independently of human activity. In recognition of this elementary fact, the IPCC defines 'climate change' and 'climate variability' with reference to (1) 'natural internal processes within the climate system', and (2) 'external forcing', which may be either natural (e.g. solar) or anthropogenic in origin. It thus draws a clear distinction,

---

[§] The Committee on Climate Change is a small high-level advisory body established by the British government. Alongside Lord Turner, it includes three professional economists among its members.

which should be observed in all serious discussion, between climate change and
AGW.‖

Going too far

In this widespread misuse of language there is typically a strong element of over-
statement, not to mention drama. Thus in all but the first of the above quota-
tions it is taken as beyond question, because emerging from 'the science', (1) that
AGW is now the dominant influence on climate change, so that for practical
purposes the terms are interchangeable, and (2) that in consequence enormous
and unprecedented risks have incontrovertibly emerged. To me, it seems unnecessary and imprudent for economists to arrive at such confident and sweeping
conclusions on matters that fall outside their subject. Further, it is going too far
to claim, or take for granted, that the two above propositions mirror agreed and
conclusive expert findings. As I see it, there are three reasons for taking a more
qualified point of departure.

The first reason is the extent of continuing and pervasive uncertainty – and,
as some would argue, sheer lack of knowledge – in relation to the climate system. In this whole disputed subject area, a proposition that all can agree on is
that the system is one of extraordinary complexity, which is far from being well
understood. one expert witness to that effect is John Zillman, formerly a leading member of the IPCC's managing Bureau (and a staunch upholder still). In
a paper published in 2005 he writes (p. 3) that:

> uncertainty pervades almost every aspect of our understanding of the cli-
> mate system... The uncertainties surrounding climate (and especially cli-
> mate change) are not limited to what will happen in the future but span
> the complete spectrum of our knowledge of past climate, and our under-
> standing of the mechanisms of present climate, to our ability to predict
> future climate.

In an earlier (2004) paper, Zillman refers to 'the large, and still largely unpre-
dictable, natural variability of climate on timescales from decades to centuries'.
This emphasis on prevailing uncertainties is a recurring theme of the instructive
report prepared for the National Research Council (NRC) of the United States,
in response to a request from President Bush, by a high-level Committee on the
Science of Climate Change (CSCC). The report was published in 2001. On my

---

‖ The reference here is to the glossary (pp. 941–954) appended to the last (AR4) report from
WGI. Garnaut (2008, p. 27) claims that his report 'uses the IPCC definition', but I could see no sign
of such compliance in his text. It is true that the Framework Convention defines 'climate change'
with reference only to the impact of AGW, but authors rarely seek to justify their language by
referring to this unfortunate usage.

count, it lists at various points twelve distinct aspects of uncertainty. All these appear as significant, and some as fundamental. It is true that, more recently, the 2007 WGI report refers to ways in which uncertainties have been reduced, but my layman's impression is that the picture as presented by Zillman and the NRC committee has changed but little; and indeed, commentators on the WGI report (Green *et al.* 2007) have made the point (p. 3) that 'the terms "uncertain" and "uncertainties" appear more than 1,300 times' in the text.

Against this background, it is misleading to speak in general terms of 'the science', in a way which suggests that there are now no significant doubts, queries or gaps. Indeed, the CSCC report specifically cautions, in the context of the IPCC's work, against '[giving] an impression that the science of global warming is "settled", even though many uncertainties still remain' (p. 22). Some if not all the committee members might endorse the position taken last year in a personal statement by a leading British climate scientist (and upholder), Mike Hulme (2008), who referred there to 'the limits and fragility of climate science'.

A second reason for due caution is that, just as with their economic counterparts, there exists a broad spectrum of views among scientific upholders: given the range and depth of uncertainties, this is only to be expected. Some of the differences relate to what can be said with confidence about the arguably dominant influence and resulting dangers of AGW. The point can be illustrated with reference to the two widely accepted propositions referred to above. As to the hypothesis that AGW can now be taken to be the principal influence on climate change, here are two contrasting views from leading American scientists, both of whom can be classed as upholders.

- James Hansen, Director of the Goddard Institute for Space Studies, has taken the position (2007) that 'Humans now control global climate' and (2008a) that 'the human-made increase of atmospheric carbon dioxide (CO_2), from the pre-industrial 280 parts per million (ppm) to today's 385 ppm, has already raised the CO_2 amount into the dangerous range'.

- Carl Wunsch, a professor of oceanography at the Massachusetts Institute of Technology, in a personal statement put out (2007) by the Royal Society writes, first, that 'We know that [the climate] is capable of remarkable changes without human intervention', and later in the text, that 'at bottom, it is very difficult to separate human induced change from natural change, certainly not with the confidence we all seek'. ¶

¶ It should be added that Wunsch goes on to say that 'It is probably true that most scientists would assign a very high probability that human-induced change is already strongly present in the climate system....'.

As to the view that risks of catastrophe have now beyond question emerged, Hansen (2008b) is indeed of the opinion that 'the climate system is danger-ously close to tipping points that could have disastrous consequences...', so that (2008a) 'our planet itself is in peril'. on the other hand, Mike Hulme, in an earlier (2006) statement than the one quoted above, spoke of 'a discourse of catastro-phe [which] is a political and rhetorical device', and identified references to 'irre-versible tipping in the Earth's climate' as one instance of this 'discourse'. He took the view that 'To state that climate change will be "catastrophic" hides a cascade of value-laden assumptions which do not emerge from empirical or theoretical science.'

This is not to say that Hansen and those who think like him are necessarily wrong on either count. The point is simply that within prevailing scientific opin-ion there are, not surprisingly, differences about the past, present and prospec-tive behaviour of the climate system and, within that system, the current and prospective impact of AGW.

A third reason is to be found in the continuing evidence of dissenting or non-subscribing views within the scientific world. recent evidence on this sub-ject is to be found, in convenient form, in the newly revised (December 2008) version of a document prepared by the office of the Republican ranking mem-ber of the Environment and Public Works Committee of the US Senate. This re-port is a kind of nonconformist anthology: it presents, through summary direct quotation, the recently expressed views of some 650 variously qualified profes-sionals, all of whom question one or more aspects of prevailing views on climate change.** Features of the document worth noting are as follows.

- A widely shared judgement is that, since 'the causes of climate change are many, various and very incompletely understood',[††] it is difficult, if not impossible, to isolate the effects of human activity.

- Many of those quoted hold the view that natural influences on the climate, as opposed to the consequences of human activity, continue to predomi-nate.

- Expressions of doubt or dissent have come from experts in related areas, such as geology and physics, and indeed meteorology, as well as climate science.

- On my count, close to 100 American meteorologists are quoted. This lends weight to the view expressed by one of them (Cohen, p. 37 of the first

---

** I have to declare an interest here, since I am one of the authors cited – though not in relation to scientific aspects.

[††] This form of words is taken from a presentation by an Australian scientist, Robert Carter.

version), who has written: 'I do not agree with all the IPCC's conclusions and know through peer discussions that the idea of a consensus in the meteorological community is false.'

The existence of informed scientific dissent is barely recognised in the various sources referred to here.

To sum up: given the huge complexity of the climate system and the large gaps in present knowledge, the unsurprising existence of a range of views among the scientific upholders, and the extent of professional doubts and dissent, generalised references to a 'scientific consensus' are out of place. It is likewise inappropriate to refer, as Helm does (2008, pp. 214, 223, 224) to what 'scientists say', 'scientists tell us' and 'scientists advise', as though there were no scientific non-subscribers and no serious differences of opinion on the upholders' side of the fence. received opinion among economists is apt to view 'the science' as monolithic and firmly established, when in fact it is neither.

Against this background, the following statements appear as too unqualified.

- Nordhaus (2008, p. xi): 'global warming will cast a shadow over the world for decades'.

- Stern Review (2007, p. xviii): 'climate change [sic] is the greatest market failure the world has ever seen.'

- Garnaut (2008, p. 592): 'We know that the possibilities from climate change [sic] include shocks far more severe than others in the past that have exceeded society's capacity to cope...'

- IMF (2008, p. 133): 'The damage from climate change [sic] and its costs are irreversible.'

- Weitzman (2009, p. 27): 'What we *do* know about climate science and extreme tail probabilities is that planet Earth hovers in an unstable trigger-prone "whipsaw" earth–atmosphere system [Hansen *et al.*, *Phil. Trans. R. Soc.* 2007, pp. 1925–54], [and that] chaotic dynamic responses to geologically instantaneous GHG shocks are quite possible...'

To these may be added the following, as a further instance from the official world.

- The International Energy Agency, in its latest (2008) *World Energy Outlook* (p. 37): 'Preventing catastrophic and irreversible damage to the global climate ultimately requires a major decarbonisation of the world energy sources.'

All the above assertions, and others like them, present as established truth what are in fact no more than arguable propositions that have found some expert support. They should all have been couched in conditional terms. Weitzman's supporting reference implies, wrongly, that Hansen's view of the world is beyond challenge. Neither Weitzman nor Garnaut is justified in using the term 'know'. Overconfidence in diagnosis has its parallel in prescription. It is widely presumed, including by the sources considered here, that the climate, as represented by global average surface temperatures, can be reliably tuned and equilibrated through judicious control of emissions. However, the causal relationships involved represent hypotheses – some would say conjectures – rather than established truth.

The tendency of many economists to take overconfident positions in relation to scientific matters has gone together with, and partly results from, a failure to take due note of evidence that the official advisory process is neither objective nor authoritative.

Inadvertence and misplaced trust

Disregarding evidence

Over the past 20 years, governments everywhere, and a great many outsiders too, have put their trust in the official advisory process as a whole and the IPCC process in particular: this is true also of majority opinion among economists. I have come to believe that this widespread trust is unwarranted. The evidence that has led me to form this view is almost wholly disregarded in the sources referred to here, largely I think through inadvertence.

In what follows I focus mainly on the IPCC process, although it is the entire official advisory process that has to be put in question. What is at issue here is not, as suggested by Stern Review authors, a matter of 'procedures' only, as distinct from substance. In so far as the established advisory process that the world relies on is not professionally up to the mark, the basis and rationale of the official policy consensus are put in question.

In July 2005 the House of Lords Select Committee on Economic Affairs, in a unanimous report, expressed (p. 6) 'concerns about the objectivity of the IPCC process'. The report was dismissed by Her Majesty's Government, and it finds no place among the 1,100 or so references in the Stern Review. However, both before and since its publication, critics have drawn attention, in my opinion with good reason, to flaws in the conduct of the IPCC process.

As noted above, it is the reports from the Panel's WGI, on climate science, that have especially carried weight and shaped received opinion. It is the more significant, therefore, that the most telling criticisms of the IPCC process have related to scientific aspects, as treated in key chapters of the past two WGI reports.[‡‡] The main thrusts of criticism have been:

- over-reliance on peer review procedures that do not serve as a guarantee of quality and do not ensure due disclosure of sources, data and procedures followed in the treatment of data

- serious failures of due disclosure and archiving in relation to studies that the IPCC has drawn on

- basic errors in the handling of data, through failure to consult or involve trained statisticians

- failure to take due account of relevant published work and evidence

- failure to take due note of comments from dissenting critics who took part in the preparation of the AR4 WGI report

- resisting the disclosure of pertinent documents, despite the formal instruction of member governments that the Panel's proceedings should be 'open and transparent'

- and, last but not least, failure on the part of the Panel and the IPCC directing circle to acknowledge and remedy the above deficiencies.

Exposure of these flaws in the process has come from a number of independent commentators, and in particular from two Canadian authors, Stephen McIntyre and Ross McKitrick: both separately and in joint presentations, they have made an outstanding contribution to public debate.[*] Their attention was initially focused on the climate reconstruction presented in the influential and much-publicised 'hockey-stick' study, which was prominently featured in the IPCC's Third Assessment Report of 2001 and thereafter. Their criticisms eventually prompted parallel initiatives by two committees of the US House of Representatives. Both committees set up high-level inquiries into the subject – one from an expert group appointed by the NRC, and the other from a team of statisticians led by Edward Wegman (Wegman *et al.* 2006), then chair of the US National Academy of Science committee on Applied and Theoretical Statistics. Both inquiries reported in July 2006. The outcome fully bears out the McIntyre–McKitrick critique, and the Wegman report is severe in its judgement on the

---

[‡‡] Helm says (2008, p. 217) that 'dissent [from IPCC conclusions] has been more heavily focused on the economics and policy aspects and less on the pure science'. This is not correct and shows a lack of acquaintance with the sources to be mentioned below (although in a passing footnote reference he mentions the Select Committee report).

[*] McKitrick's website, http://ross.mckitrick.googlepages.com, provides an annotated set of references, some of which are included in the list of references appended to this paper. McIntyre's blog, climateaudit.org, is a notable continuing source of analysis, commentary and debate.

studies involved. Other aspects of the work for WGI have also been subject to expert challenge. One such aspect concerns the instrument-based series for global average surface temperature on which the Working Group and other official sources have relied: the estimated temperature anomalies appear as subject to doubt because of imperfections in coverage and reliability, questionable statistical procedures and non-climatic influences for which full allowance may not have been made. Again, the conduct of the drafting process for key chapters of the WGI report for AR4 has been called into question. Under both these latter headings also, issues of non-disclosure have been raised, and critics have had to resort to freedom of information legislation to gain access to material which should from the start have been in the public domain.

This whole array of criticisms, and their history, are set out in two recent and notable published papers. The first, by David Holland, is entitled 'Bias and concealment in the IPCC process' (2007), while the second is by Ross McKitrick (2008).[†] Both papers, with full supporting evidence, put in question, first, the claims to authority of arguments that have been at the core of the IPCC's treatment of the scientific evidence; second, the objectivity and neutrality of leading WGI authors and reviewers; and third, any presumption that in these proceedings the peer review process provides an effective guard against bias on the part of those authors and reviewers. McKitrick's verdict on the drafting process for that report, in which he and McIntyre participated as invited reviewers, is that:

> The core writing team...shares a single point of view, that its members are alert and predisposed to evidence that confirms that point of view, and that they are unreceptive or openly hostile to evidence that contradicts it. (McKitrick 2008, p. 99).

The evidence just cited points to 'the need for comprehensive audit of the quality of the science-based information on climate risk that is currently being used by governments to set public policy' (Holland et al., 2007, p. 143). The possibility that such a need might exist is not recognised in any of the sources considered here.

Overlooking bias

What the critics have uncovered suggests a strong element of bias in some areas of climate science and among those in charge of the WGI draft. I believe that

---

[†] Holland's paper is in *Energy and Environment*, 18, 7/8 (2007), while McKitrick's piece forms a chapter in a book called *The Global Warming Debate: Science, Economics and Policy*, published in 2008 by the American Institute for Economic Research. The general problem of disclosure failure in academic work, which goes well beyond climate science, forms the subject of a recent well-documented and disturbing essay by Mccullough and McKitrick (2009).

the problem goes wider, and that a chronic and pervasive bias characterises the official advisory process as a whole.

To avoid bias and over-presumption would in fact have required a conscious and determined effort on the part of governments and the officials involved. It is true that the IPCC as such has been formally instructed by its member governments, in the 'principles governing IPCC work', that its reports 'should be neutral with respect to policy'. But the Panel members themselves, as also the senior officials they report to, are not and cannot be neutral: as government servants, they are committed, inevitably and rightly, to the official policy consensus. They stand by the objective set out in the Framework Convention and the resulting policy decisions. That is the context within which the three successive IPCC Assessment Reports prepared since 1992 have been put together by the expert network and reviewed by the Panel and its member governments. The fact is that departments and agencies which are not and cannot be 'policy-neutral' are deeply involved, from start to finish, in the preparation of the reports.

To be sure, those departments and agencies could still have made it a prime concern to ensure that the IPCC reporting process which they control remained open, balanced and policy-neutral. As I read the history, however, this has not happened. From the earliest days, members of the IPCC managing Bureau and the directing circle they form part of, like the environmental policy milieu in general, have been characterised by what Clive Crook, writing in the *Financial Times* (2 August 2006), has termed 'pre-commitment to the urgency of the climate cause'. By way of illustration here are three public statements made by top officials in February 2007, following the publication of the draft AR4 WGI report.

- Dr R.K. Pachauri, chair of the IPCC: 'I hope this report will shock people [and] governments into taking more serious action.'

- Achim Steiner, Executive Director of the United Nations Environment Programme: 'in the light of the report's findings, it would be "irresponsible" to resist or seek to delay actions on mandatory emissions cuts'.[‡]

- Yvo de Boer, Executive Secretary of the Framework Convention: 'the findings leave no doubt as to the dangers that mankind is facing and must be acted on without delay'.

These are strong assertions. All three speakers went beyond the actual WGI text, to draw their own personal conclusions as to the implications for policy. While they were fully entitled to form and air such opinions, their statements were not just summaries of 'the science', nor of course were they 'policy-neutral'.

[‡] This and the following quotation are from the *Financial Times*, 3 February 2007.

In speaking out as they did, these officials were conforming to an established pattern. like their various predecessors in office, they are committed persons; and had this not been the case, and known to be the case, *they would not have attained their leading positions within the environmental policy milieu*. They would not have sought their respective posts, nor would they have been seen by UN agencies and member governments as eligible to hold them, had they not been identified as holding strongly the view that human activities are putting the planet at risk. The advisory process is run today, as it has been from the start, by true believers. Not surprisingly, the same commitment is to be found among leading members of the IPCC expert network, with results such as have been noted above.

It is not just the IPCC process that is in question here. The basic problem of unwarranted trust goes further: it extends to the chronically biased treatment of climate change issues by responsible departments and agencies that the Panel reports to, and in nationally based organisations which they finance. It is not only in official circles, within the environmental policy milieu, that this ingrained bias is to be found. Elements within the international scientific establishment appear as strongly committed, rather than neutral and objective, in relation to climate change issues. One aspect of this strong commitment has been a readiness to condemn any form of questioning or dissent as 'undermining the science'. Again, non-subscribers have been portrayed, though with no actual evidence cited, as members of 'an active and well-funded "denial lobby"'.[§]

So far as my reading goes, these features of the handling of climate change issues have passed unnoticed in the sources considered here. The various authors take the established official process of inquiry and assessment as given, trustworthy and professionally watertight: hence they accept its 'consensus' results. In their analysis, and in the conclusions they draw for policy, there is no trace, hint, vestige or glimmer of awareness that that process could be seriously flawed, in ways that put many of its results in question. The published evidence to that effect goes unrecognised in their work.

Sanctioning a culture of conformity

As things now are, the dominance of received opinion across the whole range of official advisory bodies, and in professional circles generally, appears assured. Policy and research alike are almost entirely in the hands of bodies that can

---

[§] The words are those of Robert (Lord) May, a recent President of the Royal Society, in an article published (6 April 2007) in the *Times Literary Supplement*. The argument of this paragraph is spelled out, with supporting evidence, in Henderson (2007a, pp. 206–207 and 219–224).

be seen as firmly committed. The case of the United Kingdom is illustrative. Here the list of those involved in the advisory and policy process, and spending public money accordingly, includes the new Department of Energy and climate change, the Department of the Environment, the Ministry of Defence, the Office of Climate Change, the Committee on Climate Change, the Meteorological Office, the Hadley Centre, the Tyndall Centre, the National Environment Research Council, the Energy Research Centre, the Carbon Trust, the Environment Agency, and the Sustainable Development Commission. I do not offer the above list as conclusive, and indeed, on present evidence, Her Majesty's Treasury should be included in it.

In all these official bodies, as also in the growing number of privately supported research centres that have been set up in Britain to work on issues relating to climate change, a common way of thinking prevails. I doubt whether among them there is today, or could ever be, given present attitudes and presumptions, even a handful of professional staff members who could be identified as even mild dissenters or non-subscribers: there is no place for such minority thoughts, and no point in voicing them. Her Majesty's Government, with full support from opposition parties and a good deal of unofficial backing, has created and financed a dominant culture of conformity.‖ Most other OECD member governments, and the European Commission, have taken much the same path.

This state of affairs gives grounds for concern. There is an obvious risk that official decisions on research and development support will be chronically slanted towards confirming and reinforcing received opinion. In this context, one may note a recent statement by Robert Watson, a former chair of the IPCC, who is now Chief Scientist of the relevant British Government departments and doubtless a strong influence on the content of a large and growing research budget, that 'Sceptics who disseminate misinformation and argue that there is no need to address this urgent issue are placing the planet at risk' (*Guardian*, 21 July 2008). A related danger is that scientists across a range of relevant disciplines will increasingly be subject to what a leading climate scientist, Richard Lindzen, has referred to in a recent (2008) paper as 'pressures to inhibit inquiry and problem solving'. In this paper he provides disturbing evidence that such pressures, which take various forms. are now an established feature of the world of climate science.

Both the culture of conformity and the risks that it creates go unrecognised in the sources considered here. one such risk is that economists themselves will increasingly form part of the culture.

‖ I took this phrase from a recent lecture by Aynsley Kellow, an Australian political scientist (2008).

A failure of due diligence

It is a striking feature of the climate change debate that telling criticisms of the advisory process and some of its key findings have come from a number of independent outsiders, with apparently no counterparts in the official world where moreover their work seems to have been disregarded. Such an incurious and dismissive official stance is understandable, though hardly to be commended, in environmental departments and agencies. But in the case of the central economic departments of state – treasuries, ministries of economics and finance, and, in the US, the Council of Economic Advisers – it is harder to account for or condone. This is an area of policy in which the economic stakes, and the possible costs of mistaken policies, could be very high (more on this below). Hence a responsibility falls on those departments of state to make informed assessments of their own, and not simply to take on trust and in full the received opinions of the environmental policy milieu and its chosen instruments – even when those opinions are endorsed from the outside by eminent scientists and scientific bodies.

I am myself a former Treasury official; and, much later, as head of what was then the Economics and Statistics Department in the OECD Secretariat, I had close dealings over a number of years with economics and finance ministries in OECD member countries. I have been surprised by the failure of these ministries to go more deeply into the evidence bearing on climate change issues, their uncritical acceptance of the results of a process of inquiry that is so obviously biased and flawed, and their lack of attention to the criticisms of that process that have been voiced by independent outsiders – criticisms which, as I think, they ought to have been making themselves. A similar lack of resource has characterised the Research Department of the IMF and the Economics Department of the OECD, both of which work in close conjunction with treasuries and finance ministries.

There is here a conspicuous failure of due diligence.

A missing dimension

The combined influence of over-presumption, inadvertence and misplaced trust is reflected in a treatment of policy issues, in economists' writings and more generally, which has an important missing dimension.

First under this heading, a word of background.

The twin aspects of risk

Received opinion takes it as now established that serious risks and dangers may or will arise from AGW unless emissions are decisively curbed. Mitigation policies are widely viewed as a wise precaution, a prudent form of insurance against losses or disasters. But such policies are not costless; and the more ambitious they are, in terms of both scale and timing, the higher the prospective costs. Hence risk has twin aspects, and policy choice requires a trade-off. of course, the costs arising from mitigation policies are highly uncertain: a range of estimates can be found, some of them reassuring. For the purposes of my argument, however, it is only necessary to make the point that, just as the consequences of AGW *could* be grave, so also *could* those arising from stringent mitigation. Some considerations here are as follows.

- The scale and timing of emissions reductions proposed by even limited upholders, and already announced by some governments, would involve huge adjustments to economic systems. In particular, effective 'decarbonisation' of transport, buildings, power generation and energy-intensive manufacturing could prove a costly undertaking. More radical measures, as advocated by strong upholders, would carry greater risks of the same kind.

- Costs are affected by the choice of mitigation measures that governments make. Economists have rightly emphasised the case for a uniform 'carbon price', as distinct from the array of specific subsidies, tax incentives, mandatory targets, prohibitions and regulations that Martin Wolf, in his *Financial Times* column (16 March 2007), has aptly termed 'a host of interventionist gimmickry'. On present evidence, as noted in two of the studies referred to here, the prospects for policy packages that will keep costs in check are not good: Nordhaus writes (2008, p. 18) that 'all the policies that have been implemented to date fail…tests of…efficiency', while Helm (2008, p. 225) points to the prevalence of 'government failure, regulatory capture, and…rent-seeking behaviour'.

- It is not only through their material impact that far-reaching mitigation programmes may have worrying consequences. There is an obvious danger that they will give rise to intrusive restrictions on both freedom of action and freedom of expression; signs of both are already apparent. This danger has been underlined by the President of the czech republic, Vaclav Klaus, in a recent book (2008) entitled *Blue Planet in Green Shackles* and subtitled *What is Endangered: Climate or Freedom?*, and it forms the theme of a recent (2008) paper by Alan Peacock.

- The measures that could give rise to these serious risks might prove in the event to have served no useful purpose, since it is not to be ruled out that, in the light of further evidence and experience, AGW will cease to appear as a threat.

- Bearing in mind the above points, there is 'a non-negligible probability' (to take over Weitzman's language in relation to climate disaster) that, to quote Nigel lawson in his recent book (2008, p. 88), 'mitigation policies [could] turn out to be the greatest misuse of resources the world has ever known'.

Against this background, and in the light of arguments made above, a case emerges for an additional form of precautionary action, of a kind that so far has been largely overlooked by governments and commentators, including the sources considered here. The action would be directed towards broadening and tightening up the official process of inquiry, including the IPCC process, with a view to creating a more secure basis for policy decisions. Although it is by no means only the scientific aspects that are in question here, these deserve pride of place.

Extending due precaution

The following are instances of the kinds of action that could be taken. They are partly overlapping, and are listed in increasing order of difficulty and complexity.

Disclosure failures: Standards of archiving and disclosure in climate science should be brought into line with what leading journals in some other areas have come to prescribe. Thus for example the *American Economic Review* now requires of articles submitted, as a precondition of publication, that data and computer code, in sufficient detail to permit replication, should be archived on the journal's website. Governments should insist on full and true disclosure of sources, data and statistical procedures, as a precondition for taking published work into account in preparing the Assessment Reports; and a proviso to that effect should be written into the IPCC's terms of reference.

Handling of statistical issues: Edward Wegman, the statistician already referred to, in the course of an appearance in July 2006 before one of the aforementioned congressional committees, observed that:

> The atmospheric science community, while heavily using statistical methods, is remarkably disconnected from the mainstream community of stat-

isticians in a way, for example, that is not true of the medical and pharmaceutical communities.

This, too, is a situation that governments could remedy if they chose.

The Assessment Reports: Governments should see to it that the IPCC process actually conforms to their formal written instruction that it should be objective, open and transparent. Under this heading, Holland (2007, p. 982) provides a well-considered list of specific proposals.

Temperature data and trends: The evidence relating to the past and current behaviour of surface temperatures has been held in question in ways that should form the basis of further and continuing independent expert inquiry. In this connection, Holland (2007, p. 973) makes the point that 'no independent verification of the surface records used by the IPCC has been carried out', nor has 'full access to the computer code and data' been provided.

Auditing disaster scenarios: Some economists have been influenced by the article of Martin Weitzman (2009) already quoted. Thus Martin Wolf, in his *Financial Times* column, writes:

> I find the arguments sufficiently cogent to justify action. Above all, I find persuasive the argument of [Weitzman] that it is worth paying a great deal to eliminate the risk of catastrophe. (8 July 2008)

If however 'paying a great deal' is in question, it is pertinent to ask what has caused Weitzman to form such confident views about the possibility of catastrophe. Part of the answer is to be found in his reference (2008, p. 5) to 'A grand total of twenty-two peer-reviewed studies of climate sensitivity published in reputable scientific journals'. But as I understand it, there are other such studies not referred to by Weitzman, which have yielded substantially lower estimates of climate sensitivity. Further, and more fundamentally, it may be that Weitzman here, like Stern before him according to some of the critics of the Stern Review, has fallen into 'credulous acceptance of hypothetical, model-based explanations of the causality of climate phenomena' (Carter *et al.* 2006, p. 193). Climate models, such as those which largely underpin the studies that Weitzman refers to, deal with an extraordinarily complex system that is not at all well understood: Richard Lindzen (1992) has described them as 'experimental tools whose relation to the real world is questionable'. Before relying on them as the basis for a costly worldwide exercise in social engineering designed (to quote a leading IPCC source) 'to reshape human activities on an unprecedented scale,'[†] it would seem prudent for governments to ensure that they are systematically reviewed and evaluated by independent experts drawn from other areas. Engineering could well be one such area.

Pluralism and diversity: Given the combination of dual risks, continuing pervasive uncertainty, and the dominance of received opinion with its resulting pressures to conform, there is a case for deliberately broadening the basis of research and inquiry, including through other channels than the IPCC process – even if that process is reformed on the lines suggested above. Governments should make formal provision for eliciting a wider range of sources, opinions and expertise. So far from playing down differences of view in the interest of arriving at agreed texts, contrasting informed assessments should be commissioned, funded and published. The whole notion of aiming at a scientific consensus, rather than ensuring that rival informed views are given full expression, appears as open to doubt. The greater the perceived risks of extreme consequences, the more important it is to ensure that the advisory process is searching, thorough and inclusive, a result that mere numbers do not guarantee.

In designing and giving effect to the various measures of reform that are called for, the central economic departments of state should be closely involved.

The combined costs of all the above actions would not bulk large in relation to existing and prospective programmes of research and inquiry into climate science. In relation to the prospective costs of serious mitigation policies they are trivial. What is involved is no more than 'an "insurance policy" of spending a small amount to ensure adequate standards in the science' (Carter *et al.* 2007, p. 177). Given what is at stake, to proceed on these lines appears as common prudence. To argue the above case, for systematic independent audit and more balanced inquiry, is not to prejudge the results of these. Such a recommendation is non-presumptive: it does not entail rejection of either the official policy consensus or action to curb emissions. Since this point is not always grasped, it is worth defining more clearly the dividing line that I referred to earlier, between upholders and dissenters.

A divided profession (2)

In this connection, Garnaut in particular gives a misleading picture of professional differences. In the introduction to his Report (2008, p. xvii), he says

---

[†] The phrase is taken from an article by a former Vice-chair of the IPCC, Mohan Munasinghe (2008).

that, with the exception only of 'a small number of climate scientists of professional repute', dissenters cannot rightly be described as 'sceptics', since they 'hold strongly to the belief that the mainstream science is wrong'. This assertion has no basis, as I noted in evidence to his inquiry. There is a well-recognised difference, which Garnaut seems to have forgotten, between being an atheist and being an agnostic; and so far as my knowledge goes, it is the latter position that lay dissenters have typically chosen to adopt. Personally, and unlike some full-blown dissenters, I have never thought, said or written that 'the mainstream science is wrong'. Among other dissenting economists, Nigel Lawson, in the book already referred to, takes as his starting-point (2008, p. 5) only that 'the science of global warming is far from settled', while noting that there is 'a majority view... which can loosely be called the conventional wisdom'.

On the same page of his Report, Garnaut argues that 'the outsider to climate science has no rational choice but to accept that, on a balance of probabilities, the mainstream science is right'. But this is not a coherent position. If probabilities and not certainties are in question, then it is not irrational but appropriate to view the 'mainstream' arguments and conclusions, not as final or 'right', but rather as a collection of hypotheses which, even though they have widespread scientific backing, remain subject to further inquiry and testing. It is also reasonable to ask how far such testing is actually going on.

In their 2007 Summit Declaration, the leaders of the Group of 8 countries referred, in a section on climate change, to 'the scientific knowledge as represented in the recent IPCC reports'. Had I been a pre-Summit Sherpa, involved in the drafting of the Declaration, I would have argued strongly, though doubtless in vain, for changing 'scientific knowledge' to 'the weight of scientific opinion'. To take such a position does not involve either denying the existence or rejecting the arguments of prevailing scientific opinion.

As to policy, upholders are apt to believe, or simply presume, that dissenters necessarily favour 'inaction' or 'delay', in disregard of prevailing scientific opinion and the established policy consensus. Again, this is not correct: the true dividing line lies elsewhere. Personally, though again in contrast to some strong dissenters, I do not hold that in present circumstances action to curb emissions is unwarranted. Prevailing scientific opinion has to be given weight, as also does the related and widespread public concern at the possibility that, through rising CO_2 concentrations, 'we are meddling with very intricate processes that maintain benign conditions at the surface of this planet' (Philander 2005, p. 26). Recognising the over-presumptions and endemic bias of the advisory process for what they are does not entail saying that the official policy consensus should be ignored, rejected or overturned. In any case, the world is not starting from scratch. Governments everywhere have signed up to the Framework Convention and continued to adhere to it; and many of them have taken action, entered into commitments and created expectations accordingly. They have done so on considered expert advice which they themselves commissioned and reviewed, with strong public support and in the belief that they were acting rightly. All this cannot just be set aside overnight.

Given this whole history and the present state of affairs, I am personally inclined to favour the widespread adoption of a carbon tax (or charge), provided it can be made to work, is kept revenue-neutral and provides a basis for winding down existing forms of the costly 'interventionist gimmickry' referred to above.

Since the more limited dissenters do not start from the premise that prevailing scientific opinion is wrong, and do not necessarily reject the idea of action to curb emissions, one may ask how their position differs from that of more limited upholders such as William Nordhaus: where is the true dividing line to be drawn? The answer emerges from what has been said above, and comes under three related headings.

First, and to repeat, upholders take as a point of departure that the current influence of AGW on climate, and the dangers that it could hold for the future, have been established beyond reasonable doubt. Limited dissenters hold that this is going too far: for the time being at any rate, they remain agnostic.

Second, dissenters in general view the policy prescriptions of even limited upholders as overconfident. They do not take it as established that emissions control holds the key to regulating climate, and they question whether enough is known about the relationships involved, and the ways in which these could change, for governments to decide today on lines of action, and even supposedly binding targets, that are seen as holding good into the indefinite future. Where so much remains uncertain, unsettled or unknown, policies should be evolutionary and adaptive. If for example carbon taxes are brought in, both the appropriate rate and the case for their continuance should depend on unfolding evidence and events thoroughly and objectively assessed.** Limited dissenters hold that both the diagnosis and the prescription of the Framework Convention should be viewed, not as embodying final truth, but as working assumptions which should remain open to continued and rigorous testing and to possible reconsideration.

** Ross McKitrick has proposed (*Financial Post*, 12 June 2007, and in other places) that a carbon tax should be based on 'the mean tropical tropospheric temperature anomaly, assessed per tonne of carbon dioxide, updated annually'. The logic of this is that 'if greenhouse gases are driving climate change, there will be a unique fingerprint in the form of a strong warming trend in the tropical troposphere... climate changes due to solar variability or other natural factors will not yield this pattern: only sustained greenhouse warming will do it'. This idea for a state-contingent tax rate seems well worth looking into.

Third, and for me especially telling though rarely taken into account, there is the missing dimension. Because of their uncritical and underinformed view of the official advisory process, and disregard of its critics,

Upholders have not only taken positions that appear as over-presumptive: they have overlooked the need to strengthen the basis for policy. Governments should take prompt action to ensure that the evolution of policies is linked to a process of inquiry, review and advice that is more open, thorough, balanced and objective than is now the case. Such action would constitute a low-cost form of due precaution, with potentially high returns. The upholders have not caught on to this fact.

An alternative framework

To conclude: among economists today, both within and outside official circles, it is widely believed, or just presumed, first, that prevailing scientific opinion as to the extent and threat of AGW can no longer be seriously questioned, and second, that the established official advisory process from which that opinion chiefly emerges is objective and authoritative. This is not the right point of departure. In the handling of climate change issues generally, by economists among many others, an alternative framework is needed – less presumptive, more inclusive, more professionally watertight, and more attuned to the huge uncertainties that remain. A leading task of policy, currently unrecognised as such by many economists, should be to establish such a framework and procedures that give effect to it. Until the case for precautionary action on these lines is more widely recognised within the profession, the contribution of economists to the climate change debate will fall well short of what it could be.

References

Broome, J. (1992) *Counting the Cost of Global Warming*. Cambridge: White Horse Press.

Byatt, I., Castles, I., Goklany, I.M., Henderson, D., Lawson, N., McKitrick, R., Morris, J., Peacock, A., Robinson, C. & Skidelsky, R. (2006) The Stern Review: a dual critique, Part II: economic aspects. *World Economics*, 7, 4, pp. 199–232.

Carter, R.M., de Freitas, C.R., Goklany, I.M., Holland, D. & Lindzen, R.S. (2006) The Stern Review: a dual critique, Part I: the science. *World Economics*, 7, 4, pp. 167– 198.

Carter, R.M., de Freitas, C.R., Goklany, I.M., Holland, D. & Lindzen, R.S. (2007) Climate science and the Stern Review. *World Economics*, 8, 2, pp. 161–182.

Garnaut, R. (2008) *The Garnaut Climate Change Review: Final Report*. Australia: Cambridge University Press.

Green, K.P., Schwartz, J.M. & Hayward, S.F. (2007) *Politics Posing as Science: a Preliminary Assessment of the IPCC's Latest Climate Change Report*. American Enterprise Institute, 3 December. retrieved from www.aei.org/publications/pubID.27185/pub_detail.asp.

Hansen, J. (2007) Global warming: the threat to the planet. *Proceedings of the Leo Szilard Lecture to the American Physical Society*, Jacksonville, Fl, 17 April.

Hansen, J. (2008a) Tell Barack Obama the truth: the whole truth. retrieved from www.columbia.edu/~jeh1/mailings/20081121_obama.pdf.

Hansen, J. (2008b) Written testimony presented to a British court in support of protesters against the proposed construction of a new coal-fired power station at Kingsnorth.

Helm, D. (2008) Climate-change policy: why has so little been achieved? *Oxford Review of Economic Policy*, 24, 2, pp. 211–238.

Henderson, D. (2007a) Governments and climate change issues: the case for rethinking. *World Economics*, 8, 2, pp. 183–228.

Henderson, D. (2007b) New light or fixed presumptions? The OECD, the IMF and the treatment of climate change issues. *World Economics*, 8, 4, pp. 203–221.

Henderson, D. (2008a) Over-presumption and myopia: the IMF on climate change issues. *World Economics*, 9, 2, pp. 195–199.

Henderson, D. (2008b) Climate change issues: an Australian contribution to the debate. *World Economics*, 9, 3, pp. 217–228.

Holland, D. (2007) Bias and concealment in the IPCC process: the 'hockey-stick' affair and its implications. *Energy and Environment*, 18, 7–8, pp. 951–983.

Holland, D., Carter, R.M., de Freitas, C.R., Goklany, I.M. & Lindzen, R.S. (2007) Response to Simmons and Steffen. *World Economics*, 8, 2, pp. 143–151.

House of Lords Select Committee on Economic Affairs (2005) *The Economics of Climate Change*, Volume I: Report; Volume II: Evidence. London: The Stationery Office.

Hulme, M. (2006) Viewpoint: chaotic world of climate truth. *BBC News World*, 4 November. retrieved from http://news.bbc.co.uk/1/hi/sci/tech/6115644.stm.

Hulme, M. (2008) Five lessons of climate change: a personal statement (March). Retrieved from www.mikehulme.org/wp-content/uploads/the-five-lessons-of-climatechange.pdf.

Intergovernmental Panel on Climate Change (IPCC) (2007) *Climate Change 2007: The Physical Science Basis*. Report of Working Group I.

International Energy Agency (IEA) (2008) *World Energy Outlook*. Paris: OECD/IEA.

International Monetary Fund (2008) Climate change and the global economy. *World Economic Outlook*, ch. 4 (April). retrieved from www.imf.org/external/pubs/ft/weo/2008/01.

Kellow, A. (2008) The politics and science of climate change: the wrong stuff. Paper presented at the 2008 Harold Clough Lecture, Institute of Public Affairs, Perth, 2 October.

Klaus, V. (2008) *Blue Planet in Green Shackles. What is Endangered: Climate or Freedom?* Washington, DC: Competitive Enterprise Institute.

Lawson, N. (2008) *An Appeal to Reason: A Cool Look at Global Warming*. London: Duckworth Overlook.

Lindzen, R. (1992) Global warming: the origin and nature of the alleged scientific consensus. *Regulation*, 15, 2 (Spring), pp. 87–98.

Lindzen, R. (2008) climate science: is it currently designed to answer questions? *Proceedings of the International Symposium on Creativity and Creative Inspiration in Mathematics, Science and Engineering*, San Marino, 29–31 August. retrieved from http://arxiv.org/abs/0809.3762v3.

McCullough, B.D. & McKitrick, R. (2009) *Check the Numbers: The Case for Due Diligence in Policy Formation*. Canada: Fraser Institute.

McIntyre, S. & McKitrick, R. (2003) Corrections to the Mann *et al.* (1998) Proxy data base and Northern Hemisphere average temperature series. *Energy and Environment*, 14, 6, pp. 751–771.

McIntyre, S. & McKitrick, R. (2005a) The M&M critique of the MBH98 Northern Hemisphere Climate Index: update and implications. *Energy and Environment*, 1, 1, pp. 69–100.

McIntyre, S. & McKitrick, R. (2005b) Hockey sticks, principal components and spurious significance. *Geophysical Research Letters*, 32, 3. 88

McKitrick, R.R. (2006) The Mann *et al.* Northern Hemisphere 'hockey stick' climate index: a tale of due diligence. In: P. Michaels (ed.) *Shattered Consensus: The True State of Global Warming*. Lanham, MD: Rowman & Littlefield.

McKitrick, R.R. (2008) Response to Henderson article. In: *The Global Warming Debate: Science, Economics and Policy*. Great Barrington, MA: American Institute for Economic Research.

Munasinghe, M. (2008) Rising temperatures, rising risks. *Finance and Development*, 45, 1 (March), pp. 37–41.

National Research Council (2006) *Surface Temperature Reconstructions for the Last 2,000 Years*. Washington, DC: National Academies Press.

National Research Council (of the US National Academies), Committee on the Science of Climate Change (2001) *Climate Change Science: An Analysis of Some Key Questions*. Washington, DC: National Academies Press.

Nordhaus, W. (2008) *A Question of Balance: Weighing the Options on Global Warming Policies*. New Haven, CT: Yale University Press.

Nordhaus, W. (2009) An Analysis of the Dismal Theorem. Cowles Foundation Discussion Paper 1686, January.

Peacock, A. (2008) Climate change, religion and human freedom. In: C. Robinson (ed.) *Climate Change Policy: Challenging the Activists*. Institute of Economic Affairs. Monographs, Readings 62. London: Institute of Economic Affairs.

Philander, S.G. (2005) *Is the Temperature Rising? The Uncertain Science of Global Warming*. Princeton, NJ: Princeton University Press.

Stern, N. (2007) *The Economics of Climate Change: The Stern Review*. Cambridge: Cambridge University Press.

US Senate Environment and Public Works Committee, Minority Staff Report (Inhofe) (2008) Scientists continue to debunk 'consensus' in 2008, 11 December. Retrieved from www.epw.senate.gov/minority.

Wegman, E., Scott, D.W. & Said, Y.H. (2006) Ad hoc committee report on the 'hockey stick' global climate reconstruction, available at http://climateaudit.org/pdf/others/07142006_Wegman_report.pdf.

Weitzman, M. (2009) on modeling and interpreting the economics of catastrophic climate change. *Review of Economics and Statistics*, XCI, 1 (February), pp. 1–19.

Wunsch, C. (2007) Climate change: in my view. *Science Issues*, March, The Royal Society. retrieved from http://royalsociety.org/page.asp?id=4688&tip=1.

Zillman, J.W. (2004) Climate change: a natural hazard? Statement made at a book launch in Melbourne, Australia, 22 November.

Zillman, J.W. (2005) Uncertainty and climate change: the challenge for policy. Occasional paper 2/2005, Policy Paper No. 3, Academy of the Social Sciences in Australia.

www.ingramcontent.com/pod-product-compliance
Lightning Source LLC
Chambersburg PA
CBHW020513100426

42813CB00030B/3230/J

* 9 7 8 0 9 9 3 1 1 9 0 6 4 *